CATHOLIC LEADERSHIP
FOR CIVIL SOCIETY

A PRACTICAL GUIDE ON AUTHENTIC LAY LEADERSHIP

CATHOLIC LEADERSHIP
FOR CIVIL SOCIETY

A PRACTICAL GUIDE ON AUTHENTIC LAY LEADERSHIP

CRISTOFER PEREYRA   ERIN MONNIN

CLCS
PUBLISHERS
Phoenix, AZ

About the Authors

Cristofer Pereyra is the Chief Executive Officer for Tepeyac Leadership, Inc., a global non-profit organization dedicated to civic leadership development for lay Catholic professionals. Through its signature program, TLI, the organization provides a catalyst development experience which equips professionals to become virtuous leaders, influencing the culture and serving the common good. Pereyra's professional career started in media, when he worked for Univision Communications as a television news reporter. He is happily married, and the father of four.

Erin Monnin is a Catholic wife, mother, entrepreneur, speaker, writer, and social media influencer. As a dedicated Catholic leader and professional, her faith permeates every aspect of her life, and she sees the times we live in as a great opportunity to evangelize through our words and actions. Erin is a former FOCUS (Fellowship of Catholic University Students) missionary, a Tepeyac Leadership Initiative graduate, a Bible study leader, co-host of the "Catholic Leadership for Civil Society" podcast and blogger on multiple Catholic leadership topics.

No part of this book may be reproduced in any form or by any electronic or mechanical means, including information storage and retrieval systems, without written permission from the publisher, except by a reviewer who may quote passages in a review.

Cover Design: Amy Rodriguez

Copyright © 2022 by CLCS Publishers
www.catholicleadership.net
Phoenix

All rights reserved

ISBN: 979-8445137702

Printed in the United States of America

With gratitude

To Our Lady of Guadalupe, St. Juan Diego, St. Josemaría Escrivá, Bishop Thomas Olmsted and Archbishop José Gómez for guiding the message of this book. To Karla, Joselyn, Brandon, Gianmarco and Valeria for providing the inspiration.

Cristofer

To St. Thérèse of Lisieux and St. Joan of Arc, for their witness to the Faith which has inspired my life's work. To Joe and Brielle for believing in, supporting, and loving me in all my endeavors, especially in writing this book.

Erin

TABLE OF CONTENTS

Foreword	1
Introduction	5
Chapter 1 – "Don't leave, lead"	8
Chapter 2 – What is Leadership Anyway?	14
Chapter 3 – We Cannot All Be Theologians or Apologists	17
Chapter 4 – The Forgotten Call from Vatican II	20
Chapter 5 – Reclaiming Christendom	28
Chapter 6 – Fundamentals for Civic Leadership: Character	34
Chapter 7 – Fundamentals for Civic Leadership: Human Dignity	38
Chapter 8 – Fundamentals for Civic Leadership: Catholic Social Teaching	43
Chapter 9 – Six Fields for Civic Leadership	48
Chapter 10 – Civic Leadership in Action	59
Chapter 11 – Board Service, Where Leadership Happens	68
Chapter 12 – Excellence and Relationships	74
Chapter 13 – Work as a Service to Others	80
Chapter 14 – Called to Be Faithful	84
Chapter 15 – Identity and Purpose	88
Appendix	92
References	94

Foreword

The Church exists to evangelize. There is no other reason, no other purpose for the Church. And the Church is all of us.

For too long now people have thought the Church's mission is only a responsibility for bishops, priests and religious, or for "Church professionals" working in parishes and chanceries.

But Jesus never said that. His words are clear: Go, therefore, and make disciples of all nations, baptizing them in the name of the Father, and of the Son, and of the Holy Spirit, teaching them to observe all that I have commanded you. And He addresses these words to every one of us with no exceptions; no matter what our state in life or our "rank" in the Church.

When the great pope St. John Paul II came to America in 1987, he said: "The work of evangelization is not over. On earth it will never be over. ... The duty of carrying forward this work rests on the whole Church and on every member of the Church." Again, that means every baptized Catholic. Every one of us in the Church is called to evangelize, to be a missionary disciple, as our Holy Father Pope Francis likes to say.

In this moment in the Church's history, we are living in the "hour of the laity." Now more than ever, it is time for the lay men and lay women of the Church to burn with new desire to love Jesus and to bring His holiness and salvation to every person.

At the dawn of the first evangelization, when Our Lady of Guadalupe appeared at Tepeyac as the bright star lighting the path to Jesus for all the Americas, she did not show herself to the bishop or the priests or even to the missionaries at the time. Instead, she entrusted herself to a lay person, St. Juan Diego.

She gave him a mission: go and tell the bishop to build a church where all peoples could come to the encounter with the living God in Jesus Christ, and where they could know His love, His compassion, and His salvation.

Our Lady continues to call the laity with tender affection, speaking to your heart as your Mother, just as she spoke to Juan Diego. Our Lady is calling you to build the Church in America, to bring our neighbors to Jesus.

America is highly secularized now, and the sense of the sacred and transcendent is being lost. We are living in a time of dangerous confusion about the true meaning of human life and human freedom.

But we know that this world will not be saved by politics or technology or by all our efforts to define our own concepts of existence. Only Jesus. No other name under heaven can save us. He is the way that leads to the truth about our lives, to the love and happiness that we all long for.

We need to bring our neighbors to a new personal encounter with Jesus Christ. This was St. John Paul II's vision for the Church in America. This was the task Our Lady of Guadalupe entrusted to St. Juan Diego.

This is our vocation now. We bring others to Jesus, not only through the words that we speak, but even more, we share Jesus by the way we live. By our attitudes and actions, by the way we treat people, by the choices we make in the humble, ordinary things we do every day. At work, at home, in our friendships.

Imagine if every Catholic in America would bring just one person to an encounter with Christ. And what if each of these people would then bring one more person to Jesus? We could change America! We could change the world for Jesus!

This is how we carry out the Church's mission. Not with complicated programs or pastoral plans. But person to person, heart speaking to heart about the love of Jesus, about who He is and what He has done for us by shedding His blood on the Cross.

In this fine book, Cristofer Pereyra and Erin Monnin offer an inspiring, hopeful, and practical vision for the new evangelization of our country.

As the founder of Tepeyac Leadership Initiative, Pereyra has a deep concern for the formation of Catholic leaders who can bring the Church's principles and values to bear on their work in public life and in their professions.

I pray that this book will find a wide audience and touch many hearts.

May Our Lady of Guadalupe be near to each one of you who reads this, may she help us all to be apostles and missionary disciples, and lead many people to know the joy and newness of life that we have in Jesus Christ!

—Archbishop José H. Gomez, Archbishop of Los Angeles and President of the United States Conference of Catholic Bishops

Introduction

We need heralds of the Gospel who are experts in humanity, who know the depths of the human heart, who can share the joys, the hopes, the agonies, the distress of people today, but who are, at the same time, contemplatives who have fallen in love with God.[1]

Catholic Leadership for Civil Society was born out of the experience gained through the work of Tepeyac Leadership, Inc., a global non-profit organization dedicated to forming Catholic professionals in civic leadership. Tepeyac Leadership Inc. has a signature civic formation program, Tepeyac Leadership Initiative (TLI)—a 5-month leadership program oriented toward the development of Catholic professionals to advance the mission of the Church and serve the common good in secular society. The missions of both the organization and its signature program were the primary inspirations for us, the authors, to write this book. If you're interested in learning more, please visit tliprogram.org.

However, *Catholic Leadership for Civil Society* is independent from TLI. It's the intellectual property of us, the authors, and exists as a valuable resource on its own. We are convinced its message is urgent and timely.

We wrote this book for Catholic professionals around the world in any professional field. Because our message is action-oriented and compels the reader to execute on our vision, this book is primarily for Catholic professionals in the early to mid-stages of their careers, especially those who are ready, willing, and able to roll up their sleeves and become servant leaders in their community!

This book will also serve as a handbook for Tepeyac Leaders (graduates of TLI) to take with them as they embark on fulfilling their individual leadership commitments, a capstone component of the TLI program.

We structured this book in such a way as to give the reader the what, the why, the who and the how, exactly in that order. We hope the following chapters will:

1. Show that lay Catholic leadership is not meant to be lived within the confines of the Catholic community exclusively, but should illuminate every aspect of secular society with the Truth of the Gospel.

2. Show that lay Catholic professionals have a unique responsibility and privileged opportunity to influence the world for Christ. It's not an optional prerogative, but their duty as baptized children of God.

3. Convey that chance and coincidence are not compatible with our Catholic Faith. If God has blessed some lay Catholics with a professional career, then their career *must* become their field of mission.

4. Explore specific fields and concrete ways to carry out Catholic leadership for civil society.

Thank you in advance for the time you will invest in this book. We have endeavored to write it so it will bear much fruit in your professional and spiritual life. You are in our prayers.

Chapter 1
"Don't leave, lead"

The Lord's calling — vocation — always presents itself like this: "If any man would come after me, let him deny himself and take up his cross daily and follow me.

Yes: a vocation demands self-denial, sacrifice. But how pleasant that sacrifice turns out to be — gaudium cum pace, joy and peace — if that self-giving is complete![2]

In the wake of the horrendous abuse cases that surfaced in the summer of 2018 following an investigation led by the Pennsylvania attorney general, many Catholics were left confused and heartbroken. If you remember the atmosphere in the Church during those days, you'd recall some Catholics contemplated—and not a few proceeded to—leave the Church altogether. But in the midst of the chaos there were also brave bishops and priests, such as Fr. Mike Schmitz, who pleaded with the faithful to stay in the Church and renew it from within. In an Ascension Presents video released in August 2018, Fr. Schmitz gave the advice Catholics needed to hear: "Don't leave the Church when things get tough, *lead* the Church..."[3] It summarized well what a faithful Catholic's attitude should be when facing scandal within the Church or any other challenge. After all, this wave of scandals was not the first to surface in the Church's nearly 2,000-year history and, sadly, it's probably not the last.

The Catholic Church has never guaranteed the moral infallibility of its members at any rank of its hierarchy. What the Church has done instead is always assured the faithful of the infallibility of its teachings on faith and morals. Why? Because the Church is the custodian of the Truth as revealed by Christ and does not possess a compendium of truths of its own. Moreover, the Catholic Church has always asserted that every one of Her members is a sinner in need of repentance. That is why we have the beautiful sacrament of Reconciliation. That is why priests—even the Pope—go to confession on a regular basis. Does any of the above justify the horror of what many of us read in the infamous Pennsylvania report? No. Sexual abuse is a cancer that has no place in society, much less in the Church. In our call to prevent this and other evils from corrupting the Church, the laity must rediscover their mission. In this post COVID-19 world–full of confusion and uncertainty–and in our great need to make society a more fertile ground for the Gospel to take root, we are convinced that lay Catholic leaders are needed today more than ever. They are needed primarily in civil society.

Times have changed. Behind us are the days when the Church had such a political influence in the world that it became the supreme moral authority. It was this way in all spaces of western society, and in many other cultural traditions as well. The Catholic Church today must bring the Gospel to society in new and creative ways. We know this. We've been calling it the new evangelization for so long, it doesn't feel so new anymore. This is why Catholic laity have the special responsibility of inserting themselves into the secular world to infuse it with Truth, Goodness and Beauty—in other words, to infuse it with God. Gone are the days when we could sit back—each taking care of his own soul—while relegating to clergy and religious alone the responsibility to spread the Good News of Jesus Christ.

Though many do not yet see it, Christian civilization has imploded. It no longer exists. So, where do we go from here? There are many challenging answers to that question. One is eminent: the laity must begin to exercise tangible and effective leadership both within and—most importantly and the focus of this book—outside the boundaries of the institutional Church.

The Pope, our bishops, priests, and religious men and women simply cannot carry the weight alone, nor was it ever intended by God that they should. In the post-pandemic era, particularly in the United States, the Catholic Church finds Herself in great need of committed, faithful, lay Catholic professionals to lead in key areas of civil society. We need the laity to lead the confused outside world. It is imperative that lay leaders work on making the world friendlier to the Gospel in all areas of secular life including—and with a high degree of urgency—the legal and political fields, so that our pastors can better proclaim the Good News of Christ without obstacles.

In fact, we are of the opinion that outside the Church, the battlefield is loftier, and so are the opportunities to work for the common good while reminding the world what it seems to have forgotten, that which seems to be at the source of many of our problems today: *what it means to be a human being*. This is the main front of the cultural spiritual battle.

Imagine what the world would be like if we had more influential doctors, engineers, business owners, accountants, politicians, police officers, entertainers, etc. who were also faithful and committed Catholics. What would the world be if these laity, relying on the grace of their Baptisms and Confirmations, intentionally used their talents and meritocratically-earned positions to influence the world for Christ? Imagine how much good the laity would bring to society if we only made it a priority to use our Catholic Faith as the compass in our professional work and careers.

In the end, what the world needs more of is what the world has always needed: the world needs more saints. As Leon Bloy said, "The only real tragedy in life is to not become a saint."[4] That sure puts things into perspective! Let us strive to become saints, reflecting the image of Christ for everyone to see.

So, if you, like us, are disappointed with the things you've seen happen inside and outside the Church over the past few years or decades; if you are frustrated with the widespread corruption that seems to have only increased during the pandemic and with the continuous succession of crises today...We want to invite you to find in these pages a way to let that holy anger lead you to greater determination and a renewed commitment to the mission of the Church, concretely, through your active participation in civil society as a lay Catholic leader.

We believe that if there ever was a time when the world and the Church were in great need for lay leadership, that time is now. Archbishop José Gomez of Los Angeles, the current president of the USCCB, has asserted that this time in history is "the hour of the laity." Ours are turbulent times, and our contemporary reality cries out for holy lay leadership in all areas of life. Through our personal work for the Church under Bishop Thomas Olmsted of Phoenix, inspired by his leadership and vision, through much prayer and reflection, we have come to this conclusion: **it is imperative that the laity does its part to lead now—in and outside the institutional Catholic Church.** The Pope and the bishops carry the Magisterium and the teachings of the Church. Only they can make the sacraments available to us. This, however, is absolutely no reason why we should only expect courageous and magnanimous leadership to come from the ranks of the clergy. Let us accept the challenge and wake-up call from Archbishop Gomez. This is the hour of the laity!

Not long ago in Italy, St. Gianna Molla was a physician, a wife and a mother who defended the dignity of innocent human life. During the Cristero War in Mexico, St. Manuel Morales was a baker, husband and father, who became secretary of the local Catholic Workers Union, and president of the National League for the Defense of Religious Liberty. Servant of God, Dorothy Day, born in Brooklyn, who had committed an abortion, repented and became a social leader who started the Catholic Worker Movement. They were all lay people. So was St. Juan Diego, the indigenous man who received the apparition of Our Lady of Guadalupe leading to the conversion of millions to the Catholic Faith.

What each of these men and women had in common was more than their Catholic Faith; it was an understanding—in some ways ahead of their time—of the Church's need for lay Catholic participation in leadership in order to advance its mission. Prior to the Second Vatican Council (Vatican II), St. Josemaría Escrivá began powerfully preaching about a way of holiness for ordinary people, lay men and women. This "new" way, previously underemphasized, consisted of prayerfully and excellently following their particular lay missions in secular society as leaders. Escrivá called the laity to do this within their professional efforts, while sanctifying their work, and by simply doing so cheerfully, striving for perfection and offering everything they did to God. If we look back at our own Church history this is not a novel concept at all, but only what the early Christians knew well and lived out in their ordinary lives.

While in parts of the world today the Church is blessed with growth, we know that elsewhere She also struggles to advance Her mission. This is at least in part due to the lack of lay leadership in civil society. The laity has for too long neglected to take ownership of their role in the Church. Why? We might need an ordained priest to celebrate Mass or hear confessions, but we don't need a priest to lead a hospital, a homeless shelter, a charitable fundraising effort, the administrative functions of the Church or even the entrepreneurial aspects of any apostolate. These are often only the needs within Church-founded organizations. There is no reason why virtuous leadership exercised by the laity should be confined to life within Catholic institutions, or apostolates.

If we look at the problems in the world from the lens of our Faith, we realize that a more committed and determined laity could generate the change so desperately needed to bring Christ back to society. It is, in fact, impossible for the Pope, our bishops, priests or consecrated religious to insert themselves into secular society in such a way as to transform it from within its secular institutions and organizational structures. Only we, the laity, can do that. What Gianna Molla, Manuel Morales, Dorothy Day, and Juan Diego did for the Church were prime examples of the type of lay leadership we so desperately need today. It used to be that men and women would become leaders simply because they were Catholic—in other words, their Catholic Faith was the very reason they wanted to lead. That is no longer the case.

We feel nothing but love for and indebtedness to the priests and consecrated religious people in our lives. The clear majority of the clergy are faithful, holy people, committed to serving Christ and His Church. But these ordained and consecrated faithful need us to be who we are as laity! The time has come for the laity to step up and into the leadership role they are called to fulfill. Venerable Archbishop Fulton Sheen said it well: "Who is going to save our Church? Not our bishops, not our priests and religious. It is up to you, the people. You have the minds, the eyes, and the ears to save the Church."[5]

Chapter 2
What is Leadership Anyway?

I think it is very good that you should try daily to increase the depth of your concern for those under you. For to feel surrounded and protected by the affectionate understanding of the one in charge, can be the effective help which is needed by the people you have to serve by means of your governance.[6]

The *Oxford* dictionary offers three definitions for "leadership": 1) the state or position of being a leader, 2) the ability to be a leader or the qualities a good leader should have, 3) a group of leaders of a particular organization, etc.[7] In other words, the dictionary is of no help. It describes the destination but offers no map for the journey. If one looks at the *Real Academia Española*, the definitions are almost identical in Spanish.

Meanwhile, in the corporate world, leadership is often thought of as effective management or result-oriented guidance from one or a few enlightened—perhaps gifted—individuals. If you ask anyone about leadership in the Catholic world, they are sure to point to the highest ranks in the clergy. But still, most are only thinking of positions, not the true virtues of a leader or the betterment of humanity through their leadership.

This is why today "leadership" has become an industry in itself. Every year there are many new books for becoming a "leader," and dozens of well-groomed, charismatic folk claim to have the ultimate leadership conference, system or pathway to transform someone into a leader. But this is an ever-failing promise considering there is a lack of consensus to describe what a leader *is*. Leadership is a human thing that most of us can instinctively *recognize* but have a hard time *defining*. And something that is undefined cannot be a goal.

We subscribe to the Virtuous Leadership Institute's definition of a leader: someone who accomplishes great things by bringing out the greatness in others. A leader—as we see it and for the purposes of this book encouraging the Catholic laity—is a person of character who makes the most of the human capital under his or her care to realize great objectives. These objectives we circumscribe to anything that upholds, safeguards or guarantees the dignity of the human person. Nothing can be more important. And they can be achieved in many realms of secular human activity.

If you now begin to see the silhouette of a leader, we still need to determine how someone becomes one "who accomplishes great things." Thus, we inevitably find ourselves seeking the wisdom of our Mother Catholic Church. For someone to inspire greatness in others, that person must first have taken on the lifelong commitment of shaping his or her character by growing in virtue. It is not a matter of arrival; it is a matter of taking on the journey with intentionality. That is what others will distinctively recognize and be immediately attracted to. When people observe and appreciate the great journey a leader has undertaken, they cannot help but to be attracted to it and want to embark on it themselves, too.

We want to ignite in lay Catholic professionals a thirst for greatness. If you were looking for the way, we hope to point you in the right direction. Every lay Catholic leader's journey starts by identifying specific issues of concern in society today. These need to be studied closely from the Catholic lens. The study of the issues should be followed by prayer. It is here where the Holy Spirit will usually plant a burning desire in the leader's heart to act on a specific area. Each leader must enter this discernment process to recognize the concrete ways in which God is calling him or her to lead. From that discernment, the leader must take the time to present in front of God an

individual commitment to lead. It's a beautiful process—led entirely by the Holy Spirit—that us authors have now had the blessing of witnessing several times.
So, this is how we define *Catholic Leadership for Civil Society*—by action! Lay Catholic leaders in civil society are those Catholics who ultimately roll up their sleeves and serve, allowing God to work on each of them first, so they can then go out to accomplish great things for God's greater glory. Some might think of this vision as idealistic. We prefer to think of it as faith-filled, for the source of their Catholic leadership ultimately comes from each lay Catholic leader's identity as a follower of the greatest leader of all, our Lord Jesus Christ.

> *Great is the LORD and worthy of much praise, whose grandeur is beyond understanding. One generation praises your deeds to the next and proclaims your mighty works. They speak of the splendor of your majestic glory, tell of your wonderful deeds. They speak of the power of your awesome acts and recount your great deeds.*
> *They celebrate your abounding goodness and joyfully sing of your justice.*[8]

In the pages that follow we would like to lay out the vision for rediscovering and reinvigorating lay Catholic leadership, which we humbly bring to the feet of Our Lady of Guadalupe—inspired by the faithfulness of St. Juan Diego—and dare to call *Catholic Leadership for Civil Society*.

Chapter 3
We Cannot All Be Theologians or Apologists

Every job that is not opposed to the divine law is good and noble, and capable of being raised to the supernatural plane, that is, inserted into the constant flow of Love which defines the life of a child of God.[9]

Undoubtedly, for some Catholics, getting a degree in theology is exactly what God wants. Some might be destined for the priesthood or religious life but have not yet discovered their vocation. These people could definitely put advanced theological formation to the service of the Church. There are also those lay people made for academia—like Dr. Scott Hahn—for whom advanced studies in theology are simply a must. Then, there are other lay men and women who thrive as catechists, leading an apostolate or an evangelization effort for their diocese. For them also, advanced theology studies might be of great service to the Church.

However, if the entire body of the laity in the Catholic Church were to dedicate their lives to the academic study of the Faith, then many of us would simply not (have time to) be true to what is specifically asked of us as lay people by the nature of our vocation. The nature of the lay vocation was front and center in the renewal called for and imagined by the fathers of Vatican II.

We are not discouraging the *advanced* academic study of theology by lay people. It is fundamental that the laity have a relationship with Christ and His Church, through the frequent reception of the sacraments. We also believe that every lay Catholic must be an integral part of a parish and diocesan community, at their service whenever possible. But having a burning passion for the Faith and love for God does not necessarily equate to altering one's life or career, resulting in turning all lay Catholics into aspiring theologians, catechists, or apologists. We are not disputing every Catholic's need for continuous formation in the Faith. All Catholics must seek ongoing Faith formation throughout their lives.

Our response to these concerns is to ask "Doesn't the Church and society also need doctors, lawyers, businesspeople, accountants, nurses, engineers, social workers, communicators, and educators committed to use their professional fields as mission territory?" It is this book's mission then to propose a more complete vision of an engaged Catholic laity. We need to start thinking differently about the most effective ways in which we can serve God and His Church.

Imagine for a second: What if there were more committed lay Catholics in the professional world? Catholics are already present everywhere from the most remote corners of society all the way up to the highest spheres of power. The Catholic population in the world is now over 1.3 billion! But let's face it, while we are present virtually everywhere, what we don't have are enough *faithful* Catholics.

So often, when lukewarm Catholics have an experience of encounter or re-encounter with Christ, their first instinct is to drop everything to become a full-time minister—hence the growing number of aspiring apologists or theologians in the Church. These lay men's and women's hearts and instincts are in the right place. They want to be servant leaders. What hasn't occurred to some of those discovering or coming back to the Catholic Faith is that our legislative systems, our public healthcare, the mass media, our schools and universities are crying out for more faithful lay Catholic leadership! We are referring to intentional Catholic leadership which is exercised within the bounds of the most secular institutions.

Unfortunately, it seems that it has not dawned on the minds of many lay Catholic professionals that there are institutions and places in society that our beloved priests and bishops, precisely because of their vocation and state of life, are not able to influence.
So what does this mean in practice? How does a lay Catholic professional sanctify him or herself by sanctifying the world? Those are some of the questions we'd like to answer for you.

Before moving on to the next section, we ask you to ponder...
- In a world where some doctors and politicians are no longer defending the dignity of all human beings;
- In a world where some teachers, pastors, and even parents are violating the innocence of the children whom God has placed in their care;
- In a world where science continuously defies the perfect designs of God, making the human person a means instead of the end of its work;
- And in a world of frequent mass-shootings and terrorist attacks, in the post COVID-19 world of left/right continuous political antagonism...

Where does a lay Catholic professional have the most potential to support the mission of the Church, influence the culture, and serve the common good? After all, we are not all called to be theologians!

Chapter 4
The Forgotten Call from Vatican II

For all your learning, for all your fame, your eloquence and power, if you are not humble, you are worth nothing. Cut out, root out that self-complacency which dominates you so completely. — God will help you — and then you will be able to begin working for Christ, in the lowest place in his army of apostles.[10]

The Second Vatican Council (Vatican II) was the twenty-first ecumenical council of the Catholic Church, convened by St. John XXIII, which produced a series of constitutions, declarations and decrees to direct the life of the Church in the twentieth century and beyond. This council brought about many changes to the Church and re-emphasized the laity's mission to insert themselves into the fabric of society to renew the temporal order, and the disposition of modern civilization. It was through Vatican II that we—the laity—were called to recommit to being Catholic leaders in civil society to fulfill the Church's salvific mission.

First, we should clarify who exactly the "laity" are, using an excerpt from *Lumen Gentium*.

The term laity is here understood to mean all the faithful except those in holy orders and those in the state of religious life specially approved by the Church. These faithful are by baptism made one body with Christ and are constituted among the People of God; they are in their own way made sharers in the priestly, prophetical, and kingly functions of Christ; and they carry out for their own part the mission of the whole Christian people in the Church and in the world.[11]

As the laity, we have an extraordinarily special and unique role within the Catholic Church. Our vocation is to welcome the light of the Gospel into our lives and integrate the Truth into the work we already do and the roles we already have! The documents of Vatican II explicitly communicated how we are to live out our mission as laity, so much so that they can act as a blueprint for us to live our *lay Catholic leadership in civil society*. This just begins to answer the question posed at the end of the previous chapter, and sets the stage for the rest of this book.

If you have not read the Vatican II documents in their entirety, we strongly encourage you to do so. However, this book will review many of them. Every lay person of the Catholic Church should have an understanding of the remarkable call to us from that council. If you want to read more on your own, all the documents can be found on the Vatican's website (See Appendix).

St. John Paul II said, "Vatican II remains the fundamental event of the life of the contemporary Church; fundamental for the deepening of the richness given to them by Christ."[12]

Despite how fundamental this council was for our Church, it seems to have been forgotten by many. In the following pages we hope that our examination of the role of the laity and a rediscovery of our call to lay Catholic leadership will ultimately inspire you to action. As previously stated, this is the goal of this book—not just to provide knowledge, but to inspire action and authentic renewal in the life of the Church for the life of the world.

As we set out to answer this "forgotten call," let us pray:

Dear Heavenly Father,

I come before You today humbled by this great opportunity to respond to the call to live as a lay Catholic leader. I ask for Your guidance, mercy, and strength as I boldly pursue this virtuous leadership. Allow me to accomplish great things by bringing about the greatness in others. Instill in me a desire and thirst to draw ever closer to You in all my pursuits. Holy Spirit, lead me and guide me to hear the specific calling from Vatican II and this book, Catholic Leadership for Civil Society, *for my life.*

St. Juan Diego, pray for us.

Our Lady of Guadalupe, pray for us.

Amen.

The Vatican II documents are rich with text on God's call to the laity. We will introduce and explore three of them in this chapter—*Dei Verbum, Lumen Gentium,* and *Apostolicam Actuositatem*—and briefly introduce a fourth—*Gaudium et Spes*—from which we will share inspiration throughout the rest of this book.

Let's dive in!

Dei Verbum

Dei Verbum is the Dogmatic Constitution on Divine Revelation promulgated by Pope Paul VI on November 18, 1965. This document sought "to set forth authentic doctrine on divine revelation and how it is handed on, so that by hearing the message of salvation the whole world may believe, by believing it may hope, and by hoping it may love."[13]

This constitution reminds us that, first and foremost, any good and moral calling we receive that is ordered towards the salvation of souls comes from God, and His revelation to us. It reminds us also that God handed *everything* on to us through the Apostles, everything that we need to live a life like the saints, that can land us in heaven with Him for eternity.

Now what was handed on by the Apostles includes everything which contributes toward the holiness of life and increase in faith of the peoples of God; and so the Church, in her teaching, life and worship, perpetuates

> *and hands on to all generations all that she herself is, all that she believes.*[14]

God asks us to spend our lives getting ourselves and others to Heaven because He loves us beyond all measure and wants to spend *forever* with us. He has given us everything, including our very lives, the best and most valuable gift of all!
Seriously, stop and think about that for a moment. God created us so that He could spend forever with us.

As we continue to read and learn from the Vatican II documents, let us remember God's Hand in all of it. Everything good, true, and beautiful comes from Him and Him alone. While Scripture has pride of place, God uses countless texts and things to speak to us, so that the message of salvation may be heard and received.

> *In His gracious goodness, God has seen to it that what He had revealed for the salvation of all nations would abide perpetually in its full integrity and be handed on to all generations.*[15]

Lumen Gentium

Lumen Gentium is the Dogmatic Constitution on the Church promulgated by Pope Paul VI on November 21, 1964. This document provided a fundamental understanding of the Catholic Church and reaffirmed that the Church was the same Church Jesus Christ had handed on to Peter and the Apostles.

Lumen Gentium is a rather bold document that reaffirmed, confirmed and restated the truths of the Catholic Church and our role in proclaiming those truths. As members of the Catholic Church, reading this document helps us understand and step into our role as Christ's disciples. It extends the invitation God already has for us to participate in the salvific mission of the Church and encourages us to seek and to build His kingdom in everything we do.

To be a disciple of Christ means to live your life as a response to the Great Commission, "Go, therefore, make disciples of all nations, baptizing them in the name of the Father, and of the Son, and of the holy Spirit, teaching them to observe all that I have commanded you. And behold, I am with you always, until the end of the age."[16]

God, through *Lumen Gentium*, invites us again to be His disciples.

> *Therefore all the disciples of Christ, persevering in prayer and praising God...must bear witness to Christ and give an answer to those who seek an account of that hope of eternal life which is in them.*[17]

In reading this excerpt, we understand that through prayer and nurturing our personal relationship with God, we can more fully testify to the Truth and lead others to it. This is discipleship.

In responding to the Great Commission, to discipleship, we participate in "the salvific mission of the Church."

> *The lay apostolate...is a participation in the salvific mission of the Church itself. Through their baptism and confirmation all are commissioned to that apostolate by the Lord Himself. Moreover, by the sacraments, especially holy Eucharist, that charity toward God and man which is the soul of the apostolate is communicated and nourished. Now the laity are called in a special way to make the Church present and operative in those places and circumstances where only through them can it become the salt of the earth* (Col. 1:15). *Thus every layman, in virtue of the very gifts bestowed upon him, is at the same time a witness and a living instrument of the mission of the Church itself 'according to the measure of Christ's bestowal.'* (Eph. 4:7)[18]

Christ gave us the sacraments to nourish our souls, and bestowed on each of us gifts, so that we can carry out the Church's mission of salvation for all. With all that He has given us, we are fully equipped to carry out this mission and profoundly engage in the affairs of our times to order them rightly.

> *But the laity, by their very vocation, seek the kingdom of God by engaging in temporal affairs and by ordering them according to the plan of God. They live in the world, that is, in each and in all of the secular professions and occupations. They live in the ordinary circumstances of family and social life, from which the very web of their existence is woven. They are called there by God that by exercising their*

proper function and led by the spirit of the Gospel they may work for the sanctification of the world from within as a leaven. In this way they may make Christ known to others, especially by the testimony of a life resplendent in faith, hope and charity. Therefore, since they are tightly bound up in all types of temporal affairs it is their special task to order and to throw light upon these affairs in such a way that they may come into being and then continually increase according to Christ to the praise of the Creator and the Redeemer.[19]

For all intents and purposes from here on out, the "temporal" order (or "temporal affairs," as is used in the above quote) will be discussed as the ways in which our secular society approaches the affairs of the modern world. We—the laity—have been entrusted with engaging in these affairs and ordering them towards God's plan. We have the great blessing of bringing the Gospel message to the corners of the world where it is highly important—the workplace, the home, our social networks, and the public square. These are perhaps the most difficult places to be witnesses to the Truth, yet with the strength and guidance of the Holy Spirit, we can sanctify "the world from within as leaven."[20] It is about making Christ known through our testimonies and the faith, hope and love we exemplify.

Apostolicam Actuositatem

Apostolicam Actuositatem is the Decree on the Apostolate of the Laity promulgated by Pope Paul VI on November 18, 1965. This document ultimately states that the laity need to play a more active role in the Church and the world.

Apostolicam Actuositatem doesn't just urge us to play a more active role in the Church and the world. It shows us how this can be done.

The most holy council, then, earnestly entreats all the laity in the Lord to answer gladly, nobly, and promptly the more urgent invitation of Christ in this hour and the impulse of the Holy Spirit...Through this holy synod, the Lord renews His invitation to all the laity to come closer to Him every day, recognizing that what is His is also their own (Phil. 2:5), *to associate themselves with Him in His saving mission. Once again He sends them into every town and place where He will come (cf. Luke 10:1) so that they may show that they are co-workers in the various forms and modes of the one apostolate of the Church, which must be constantly adapted to the new needs of our times. Ever productive as they should be in the work of the Lord, they know that their labor in Him is not in vain (cf. 1 Cor. 15:58).*[21]

First of all, we must recognize that without our "yes," people may miss out on hearing the message of salvation. Think about this for a moment. The opportunities to help advance the mission of the Church as a Catholic leader in civil society that you pass up on could mean souls having one less chance to spend the rest of eternity with Christ. So, let us stand up and speak up for the Truth!

For there are many persons who can hear the Gospel and recognize Christ only through the laity who live near them.[22]

Secondly, Christ has given us this specific mission because we are the right ones for the job! Bishops, priests, sisters and other religious simply can't reach the communities and the people that we can. By sharing our testimony with our peers, we can have a profound impact.

The apostolate in the social milieu, that is, the effort to infuse a Christian spirit into the mentality, customs, laws, and structures of the community in which one lives, is so much the duty and responsibility of the laity that it can never be performed properly by others. In this area the laity can exercise the apostolate of like toward like. It is here that they complement the testimony of life with the testimony of the word. (cf. Pius XI, encyclical "Quadragesimo Anno," May 15, 1931) It is here where they work or practice their profession or study or reside or spend their leisure time or have their companionship that they are more capable of helping their brethren.[23]

Third, in living a Christian life and sharing our testimony with others, we must be authentically generous. People are ever-conscious of whether our generosity is a means to an end or we are imbued with a genuine, Christian generosity.

Another requisite for the accomplishment of their task is a full consciousness of their role in building up society whereby they strive to

> *perform their domestic, social, and professional duties with such Christian generosity that their manner of acting should gradually penetrate the whole world of life and labor.*[24]

Finally, as we draw closer to Christ and take part in His saving mission, we should have unity always on our minds. Christ does not ask us to speak Truth in a way that divides us from our brothers and sisters. He calls us to meet them where they are at, find commonality and move forward together on a path towards Truth. It is not always easy, but it can be done. Not everyone is going to respond to the Truth in charity. We can be that example of Christ's love for them.

> *...the spirit of unity should be promoted in order that fraternal charity may be resplendent in the whole apostolate of the Church, common goals may be attained, and destructive rivalries avoided.*[25]

Gaudium et Spes

Gaudium et Spes is the Pastoral Constitution on the Church in the Modern World promulgated by Pope Paul VI on December 7, 1965. This document breaks down several topics—human dignity, marriage, community, culture, economic development, politics, peace and more—in which the members of the Church are always called to act. As mentioned, we will share much inspiration from this document in the chapters that follow.

The Vatican II documents provide an incredible guide for Catholics everywhere. The mission for the laity is clear and we see just how important we are to the fabric of the Church and society. Our unique position allows us to bring the Church's truths to the world and the world's brokenness to Christ. Let us not forget the call from Vatican II, but rather use it as the blueprint for our Catholic leadership in civil society.

Chapter 5
Reclaiming Christendom

Do the birds feel the weight of their wings? If you were to cut them off and put them on the scales you would see that they are heavy. But can a bird fly if they are taken away from it? It needs those wings and it does not notice their weight, for they lift it up above other creatures.

—Your "wings" are heavy too! But if you did not have them you would fall into the filthiest mire.[26]

At this point you may be thinking, *All of this sounds great in theory! But have you taken a look at the state of our world lately? It's in shambles! There's so much work to be done. Where do I even begin?*

Faithful Catholics have grown accustomed to complaining about the current state of the world, and the problems within and outside the Church. We might well be standing among the ruins of Christendom, the worldwide body and society of Christians, the Christian world. The Church remains, but beside it we find the ruins of a once thriving Christian civilization. That civilization many of us mourn was built with faith and hard work. Does our complaining do any good for the world, our Church or the Church's mission within the world? No, it does not.

We don't need to spend time listing all of the problems in the Church and in our world. We are living through them. We see them unfold before our eyes daily. And often when we think it can't get any worse, it does. It's easy to put the blame on the people, organizations and ideologies creating the chaos that is bringing society further and further away from the Truth of Jesus Christ. While we should certainly hold them accountable for their immoral actions, blaming and pointing fingers gets us nowhere. If we really want to reclaim Christendom and change the world, what is needed are more fervently faithful Catholics who not only believe in and practice the Church's teachings, but stand up for them and refuse to accept the lies that have permeated our world. We need faithful Catholics who don't spend time complaining but rather choose to take action.

While Jesus was on earth, He showed us exactly what to do. He taught us how to pray, work hard, and be so determined to testify to the Truth even if it leads to death. Prayer, along with hard work and determination, are the recipe to reclaim every area of human society for Christ.

> *...let there be no false opposition between professional and social activities on the one part, and religious life on the other. The Christian who neglects his temporal duties, neglects his duties toward his neighbor and even God, and jeopardizes his eternal salvation. Christians should rather rejoice that, following the example of Christ Who worked as an artisan, they are free to give proper exercise to all their earthly activities and to their humane, domestic, professional, social and technical enterprises by gathering them into one vital synthesis with religious values, under whose supreme direction all things are harmonized unto God's glory.*[27]

Prayer

When we receive the Eucharist at Holy Mass, this is the most intimate encounter we have with the Lord, and the closest that we can ever be to Him until we are with Him in heaven. Along with receiving the Eucharist and receiving the other sacraments, prayer is how we encounter God in a deep and profound way. It is the result of a belief in a personal God.

For many people, it seems as though daily prayer has become something to "check off the list," as if it's just another *thing* to do. And as long as it gets done, we can feel good about ourselves "living out our Faith." If you feel called out right now, that is okay. Many people struggle with this mentality when approaching prayer. You are not alone.

The good news is that Christ taught His disciples how to pray and we can learn a great lesson from His example. The Gospel of Luke regularly presents Jesus at prayer at important points in His ministry—at His baptism, at the choice of the Twelve, before Peter's confession, at the transfiguration, when He teaches His disciples to pray, at the Last Supper, on the Mount of Olives, on the cross.

In Luke 3:21, after Jesus and the crowds had been baptized by John, Jesus prayed and "heaven was opened." He shows them that **prayer is powerful**.

In Luke 5:16, Jesus withdrew to "deserted places" to pray, despite crowds who had assembled to listen to Him. In reading this, our first inclination is to think Jesus is being selfish. Here are all these people who want to hear the Good News, but He cowers away to go be alone and pray. Instead, Jesus is teaching us something incredible. He knows that He cannot do anything without His Father's help. Jesus, the Son of God, humbles Himself before the Father in prayer because He understands obedience. Through this, He teaches us that we are to humble ourselves in obedience before the Father before everything we do (no matter how big or small). **This is how we are to pray.**

In Luke 6:12, Jesus went to the mountain to pray and "spent the night in prayer to God." Read that again. *Jesus spent the entire night praying to God the Father*. He understood something that many of us don't—living out the mission of the Church, the mission God calls us to, cannot be done without Him. If we read on in this passage, we realize that He spent this night in prayer before choosing the Twelve Apostles. **If Jesus, who is God, spent countless amounts of time in prayer for His ministry, we can do the same for our own missions and apostolates.**

These examples, and a great number of others from the Bible, give us exactly what we need to understand that prayer is a gift, and that it is the important first step in reclaiming every area of human society for Christ! As lay Catholic leaders in civil society, prayer is how we are to begin reclaiming Christendom.

Hard work

We don't have to look very hard in the Bible to realize that Jesus had His work cut out for Him. God the Father sent His only Son to earth to claim Christendom thousands of years ago, just as He calls us to reclaim it now.

> *Then Jesus said to his disciples, 'Whoever wishes to come after me must deny himself, take up his cross, and follow me. For whoever wishes to save his life will lose it, but whoever loses his life for my sake will find it.*[28]

Christ never said it would be easy. Instead, He said that it would be difficult to follow Him. But the reward for following Him is the most extraordinary reward a human being can ever gain, and that is to be with Him in heaven for eternity.

At the beginning of this chapter, we talked about modern faithful Catholics complaining about the state of the world and recognizing the reality of the many problems set before us. It is true that the situation we find ourselves in can be discouraging. It seems like everywhere we look, every area of society, is plagued by the Devil and his lies—the family unit, government, education, healthcare, business, the nonprofit sector, the list goes on. Instead of seeing this as impossible to overcome, what if we saw it as a great opportunity?

> *Since all these things are so, the modern world shows itself at once powerful and weak, capable of the noblest deeds or the foulest; before it lies the path to freedom or to slavery, to progress or retreat, to brotherhood or hatred. Moreover, man is becoming aware that it is his responsibility to guide aright the forces which he has unleashed and which can enslave him or minister to him.*[29]

Brothers and sisters, we have set before us an opportunity to reclaim Christendom and change the world. Our world is desperate for and longing for the Truth. But not enough people are proclaiming it. It will be hard work. It will be challenging to keep going. It will be countercultural. But there is amazing news:

> *The Church firmly believes that Christ, who died and was raised up for all,(cf. 2 Cor. 5:15) can through His Spirit offer man the light and the strength to measure up to his supreme destiny... The Church also maintains that beneath all changes there are many realities which do not change and which have their ultimate foundation in Christ, Who is the same yesterday and today, yes and forever.(cf. Heb. 13:8)*[30]

Determination

The biggest threat our world faces is that many people have the false belief that we, as humans, can dictate the Truth to God, our Creator. This calls for an extreme determination on behalf of all faithful Catholics to reclaim the Truth of our Faith within the Church and then to go out into the world and do the same.

How can we be so determined to do this when it seems as though every corner of human society wants nothing to do with our Faith or us?

Think about Jesus' ministry for a moment. He was the only divine person ever to walk this earth, and He had a divine mission from God Himself. His ministry boiled down to this: Jesus spent three years camping and traveling with twelve men. Jesus simply spent time with people. His life was His ministry. Drawing from the example set by Christ, being determined to reclaim Christendom in today's world should look similar to His ministry. Thessalonians 2:8 says, "With such affection for you, we were determined to share with you not only the gospel of God, but our very selves as well, so dearly beloved had you become to us."

Christ calls us to be determined to spend time with people and share life with them. This is where everything else flows from.

When we earn others' trust, they are open to hearing what we have to say. Yes, even what we have to say about the Gospel.

Instead of looking at the world and despairing or complaining, as lay Catholic leaders, we can look at the world and see a wonderful opportunity. The world needs to hear the Truth. We know the Truth and can allow God to help us share it! Through prayer as Jesus taught us, hard work with our eyes fixed on eternity in heaven, and determination to share our very selves with those around us, we have what it takes to reclaim the world for Christ. We *can* do this! As we set forth on this mission, let us remember:

The Lord is the goal of human history, the focal point of the longings of history and of civilization, the center of the human race, the joy of every heart and the answer to all its yearnings.[31]

Chapter 6
Fundamentals for Civic Leadership: Character

Compromise is a word found only in the vocabulary of those who have no will to fight — the lazy, the cunning, the cowardly — for they consider themselves defeated before they start.[32]

Certain fundamental virtues are required to bring Christ back to the spaces of secular life from where He has been largely exiled. These same virtues are required to become civic leaders who participate in God's plan to renew the temporal order. Virtues build character. Many things make a Catholic leader, but a lifelong commitment to the development of one's character, demonstrated by one's intentional struggle to grow in virtue is the basis of Christian leadership. In his book *Virtuous Leadership*, Alexandre Havard writes that only a Christian who has worked to grow in the four cardinal virtues can then build upon them, and grow in the two virtues that are proper to the leader: humility and magnanimity.

Today's so-called progress often comes in the form of new answers to very old questions. At times it seems humanity seeks change for the sake of change, forsaking along the way the most zealously guarded treasures of its forefathers. That same humanity can make inadequate attempts at rediscovering its lost treasures by giving them different forms, thus unnecessarily obscuring and obstructing their true purpose and full value. The growing self-help aisle at our online bookstores is a good example of that. Even in this postmodern world, people have an urgent need to tend to their spirit. But in a world that rejects the idea of God or organized religion, the spirit's nurturing must necessarily be reduced to a caricature of what was once an effective program for fulfillment, joy, and real peace on Earth: one's lifetime growth in virtue and character.

Today, people subscribe to pay lots of money for new-age practices, such as mindfulness, in order to "pay attention to the present moment." Mindfulness is described as the art of "being self-aware," guided by meditation practices that pay close attention to one's thoughts and emotions. It follows a long line of practices that have grown and diminished in popularity at different times over the past few decades (i.e., yoga, reiki, etc.).

Today's mindfulness enthusiasts attempt to reduce their levels of stress, increase focus and/or regulate their emotions, empathy, or resilience. All of these are noble aspirations. But through the centuries—at least in the western world—we had already advanced far in this area through the Christian practices of prayer, examination of conscience, and mortification (that's right, mortification). All of these were pieces of a puzzle that culminated in the cultivation of true ladies and gentlemen. We are not making any references here to titles of nobility. Rather these words became the descriptors of Christian men and women who had been raised or strived to grow in character through the practice of virtue. Much like bodybuilders do today with their muscles, they exercised the good habits that make for good (virtuous) men or women.

Our spiritual forefathers, those who lived in a time when Christendom was fully alive, were way ahead of today's mindfulness. They knew what it meant to be self-aware. They also understood how to increase focus and better regulate their own emotions. Yesterday's Christians knew that the key to a fulfilling life was growth in virtue. And thus, they started every day with prayer and saw each day as an opportunity to become a better version of themselves through practice.

Prayer

The first prayer in a Christian's day was called the morning offering. It was the practice of dedicating the day and all its fruits to God. This early prayer accomplished something very important for believers. It started their day with the right mindset, a commitment to exemplary behavior. So each day started with self-awareness. The rest of the day would then be punctuated by prayer—the Angelus at midday, the Rosary, a short prayer before every meal, and several instances of meditation that Christians called "contemplation." These were all opportunities for self-awareness. This routine provided Christians a reminder of who they were in relationship to their Creator. It also reminded them of everything they had to be grateful for, and of their own gifts and shortcomings in character.

Examination of Conscience

The Christians of long ago would then end each day with something called an "examination of conscience." This was nothing more than the daily habit of going through a mental list, typically at night, that would cover each aspect of one's life, focusing on areas of weakness, areas where further growth in virtue was necessary. An examination of conscience would be followed by an Act of Contrition, in which Christians would ask for forgiveness for the wrongdoings of the day, and for strength with a renewed commitment to do better the next day.

A daily examination of conscience was further strengthened by the practice of going to Confession and regular spiritual direction. The inhabitants of Christendom did not need to write big fat checks to a personal coach to fix their lives. They simply sought the guidance of a priest. A monthly, or sometimes weekly, visit to a priest allowed Christians to relieve themselves of the heavy weight their worst mistakes had placed on their shoulders. They called this Reconciliation. In addition, Christians would seek advice from their priest for further growth in virtue. The priests would draw inspiration and examples from Scripture or the lives of the saints. All of this helped believers be more aware of who they were, and what they were called to be. They referred to it as holiness.

Mortification

One of the most effective tools Christians used so they could live in the present moment and be more aware of their thoughts and emotions was the practice of mortification. Mortification borrowed heavily from the life of Christ and provided a path for growth in virtue by drawing from ordinary pain and suffering. Perhaps the most mystical aspect of Christianity and the most misunderstood, the practice of mortification capitalized on the reality of human pain and turned it around by transforming suffering into something of transcendental value.

Christ had already shown Christians that the glory of His Resurrection came only after the pain of His Crucifixion. And so, the Christians of long ago took those ordinary occasions of anger, sadness, and frustration—inescapable aspects of the human experience—and offered them up as sacrifice. They learned to embrace suffering with patience and meekness, even joy. Christians realized that every time they responded this way to their daily struggles, they became stronger and more virtuous. In time, they learned to habitually seek out small acts of sacrifice that they could offer up in order to continue their growth in virtue, especially in the areas of self-control, courage, prudence, and justice. Our spiritual forefathers did not need a mindfulness program in order to be mindful. They had something better. They had God.

As we continue to watch the postmodern world try to reinvent the wheel in different shapes, such as with this trend of mindfulness, we can take comfort in knowing that the wheel is round. Most importantly, if we know who we are—children of God—and what we were made for—Heaven—it will be easier to avoid taking supposed shortcuts. Through the grace of God and a predisposed will, lay Catholic leaders today can and must grow in virtue as they commit to the lifelong project of building a strong and virtuous character. For a Christian, this is the only way.

Chapter 7
Fundamentals for Civic Leadership: Human dignity

You are in a position of authority and you go by what people say? You are a doddering old man! —First of all you should worry about what God will say; then, very much in the second place, and sometimes not at all, you may consider what others might think. "Whoever acknowledges me before men", says the Lord, "I too will acknowledge him before my Father who is in heaven. But whoever disowns me before men, I will disown him before my Father who is in heaven."[33]

As leaders seeking to build the kingdom of God and renew the temporal order, we must invest in our formation with the goal of attaining a solid understanding of human dignity. Only when we truly embrace our own dignity and the dignity of others can we really be leaders in civil society. Who are we? Where does our dignity come from? What threatens human dignity? We believe that no matter where you are on the spectrum of having a clear understanding of the Church's teaching on the dignity of all life, you can learn something from what we will share in this chapter.

Often, when we are asked to describe ourselves, some of the first things that come to mind are our job titles, our role as parents, our characteristics, etc. What if the normal way to answer that question was our identity as beloved children of God? Each of us is a beloved son or daughter of God, the Father and Creator of all. That is who we are and who we always will be. No one can reject that truth or take it away from us. Genesis 1:27 says, "God created mankind in his image; in the image of God he created them; male and female he created them."

God loves us so much that He created us in His image. He could have made us into anything, but He chose to make us His to love Him and be loved by Him. We are human beings made by the Creator of the universe and we have dominion over all other creatures. As the *Catechism of the Catholic Church* says, God's plan for us is good.

God, infinitely perfect and blessed in himself, in a plan of sheer goodness freely created man to make him share in his own blessed life.[34]

God freely created us in a plan of sheer goodness. This is who we are and this is where our dignity comes from. We are innately good because we came from Goodness Himself. Let that sink in. Genesis 1:31 reiterates this, saying, "God looked at everything he had made, and found it very good."

Our dignity comes from God Himself. As soon as we are formed in our mother's womb, at the moment of conception, we have dignity. We are worthy of love, respect, honor, and all things good. We have value. We are imbued with this human dignity forever. The Book of Psalms and the Book of Jeremiah offer some beautiful truths about this.

You formed my inmost being; you knit me in my mother's womb. I praise you, because I am wonderfully made; wonderful are your works![35]

For I know well the plans I have in mind for you—oracle of the Lord— plans for your welfare and not for woe, so as to give you a future of hope.[36]

We were created by Love, for Love, to love. When we recognize this human dignity within ourselves and others, life becomes so much better and more glorious. We can fully embrace our identity as children of God and help others come to know this truth. Living this way is empowering, freeing, and so beautiful. It's the way God intended for us to live. Unfortunately, there are countless attacks on the dignity of the human person in our modern world. God's resounding Truth about who we are has become muted by society. We face many lies and threats.

To be the leaders that God is calling us to be, it is not only imperative that we understand the truth of who we are and where our dignity comes from, but also the contemporary threats to human dignity. We must be aware and vigilant so that our voices can rise up and speak the Truth into a broken world. As with many of the things we've discussed already in this book, let us not see this situation as something to be discouraged about, but rather an incredible opportunity to infuse the Truth into a society that is so desperately in need of it. In the words of St. John Paul II—inspired by St. Gabriel's words to the Blessed Virgin Mary at the Annunciation—let us "Be not afraid!"

The dignity of the human person has been under attack ever since the Devil entered the Garden of Eden. From that point on, God's perfect and beautiful plan for humanity would be stained by sin. Perhaps the greatest sin and scandal of human history is that certain people, groups and organizations think they have the right to strip people of their human dignity, and deny their very identity as beloved children of God. We've seen this happen throughout history in times such as the Holocaust, slavery, etc. and in modern times through abortion, euthanasia, assisted suicide, etc.

Although he was made by God in a state of holiness, from the very onset of his history man abused his liberty, at the urging of the Evil One. Man set himself against God and sought to attain his goal apart from God. Although they knew God, they did not glorify Him as God, but their senseless minds were darkened and they served the creature rather than the Creator. (cf. Rom. 1:21-25) What divine revelation makes known to us agrees with experience. Examining his heart, man finds that he has inclinations toward evil too, and is engulfed by manifold ills which cannot come from his good Creator. Often refusing to acknowledge God as his beginning, man has disrupted also his proper relationship to his own ultimate goal as well as his whole relationship toward himself and others and all created things.[37]

There are *many* threats to human dignity today. Our dignity is jeopardized from the moment we become human until the moment we die. Let us recall that every single person is created in God's image and in a plan of sheer goodness. But, because of the Devil's entry into human history, sin entered the world and tempts us every day to turn our back on God and His will for us. The threats to human dignity that we face today are a tragedy that we must be aware of and alert to. Innocent humans in their mother's wombs are killed every day in the United States and throughout the world. Adults and the elderly are killed through euthanasia, assisted suicide, and other ways. And between when life begins and when life ends, we witness other kinds of attacks on human dignity, such as domestic violence, racism, prostitution, our human rights being diminished or taken away, and so much more. These acts show just how ugly sin is and how human life and dignity has become something that can be trifled with.

> *Only in freedom can man direct himself toward goodness. Our contemporaries make much of this freedom and pursue it eagerly; and rightly to be sure. Often however they foster it perversely as a license for doing whatever pleases them, even if it is evil. For its part, authentic freedom is an exceptional sign of the divine image within man. For God has willed that man remain 'under the control of his own decisions' (cf. Sir. 15:14), so that he can seek his Creator spontaneously, and come freely to utter and blissful perfection through loyalty to Him. Hence man's dignity demands that he act according to a knowing and free choice that is personally motivated and prompted from within, not under blind internal impulse nor by mere external pressure. Man achieves such dignity when, emancipating himself from all captivity to passion, he pursues his goal in a spontaneous choice of what is good, and procures for himself through effective and skillful action, apt helps to that end. Since man's freedom has been damaged by sin, only by the aid of God's grace can he bring such a relationship with God into full flower. Before the judgment seat of God each man must render an account of his own life, whether he has done good or evil. (cf. 2 Cor. 5:10)*[38]

As Catholic leaders in civil society, we have the duty to properly form our understanding of human dignity in all of its facets and implications. It falls outside the scope of this book, and we simply couldn't examine each one of them, such as those contained within St. John Paul II's teachings of Theology of the Body. Ultimately, we have the right to exercise freedom of religion and freedom of speech to bring others into the fullness of truth about our dignity and the dignity of everyone around us. Not only do we have the right, but the duty to do so. "Being pro-life doesn't end at the voting booth, with a social media post on respecting the unborn, attending the March for Life, or even in serving in post-abortive healing retreats. All of these are important ways [to] work toward building a culture of life, but being pro-life extends to...daily professional life as a Catholic. Being pro-life is about orienting yourself to the dignity of the person before you."[39] Exercising the "sheer goodness" that God created us from, let us approach our lives and the lives of others as great gifts to be thankful for and blessed by. Only then can we begin to build a culture where the human dignity of *all* is upheld.

Chapter 8
Fundamentals for Civic Leadership: Catholic Social Teaching

As soon as you truly abandon yourself in the Lord, you will know how to be content with whatever happens. You will not lose your peace if your undertakings do not turn out the way you hoped, even if you have put everything into them, and used all the means necessary. For they will have "turned out" the way God wants them to.[40]

Our third and final fundamental for civic leadership, a powerful toolbox, a compass, for us as Catholic leaders is a grounded understanding of Catholic Social Teaching. The Church's social doctrine offers an integral approach to human society. Along with the teachings of Vatican II, we would argue that Catholic Social Teaching is the bread and butter of Catholic leadership for civil society. You may be very familiar with these teachings, or you may have heard the terms before but don't understand what they're referring to. Many Catholics don't realize how blessed we are to have a guide on almost all matters of human activity. Throughout this book, our hope is always to share with you the beauty and resources the Catholic Church has given its members and the world so as to foster joy, gratitude and wonder about our Faith. The Catholic Church is not outdated and unaware. Rather, She is immersed in our culture and has answers based in Truth for much of what the secular world experiences. It's time we look to the Church, which truly has our best interests and the common good at heart, rather than to the world, for help, guidance and answers as leaders in civil society.

Before we go any further, let us first define what Catholic Social Teaching is. Catholic Social Teaching is a central element of our faith, founded on the Truth of what God has revealed to us about Himself, which "seeks to proclaim the Gospel and make it present in the complex network of social relations."[41] Catholic social doctrine is presented in the documents and writings, based on the Bible and the traditions of the Church, in which Catholic Social Teaching is found. It is two-fold: (1) "it means [to infuse] into the human heart the power of meaning and freedom found in the Gospel"[42] and (2) it offers an incredible guide on how to conduct ourselves in a moral way in all matters of society so as to promote the common good of all.

There are twenty-five foundational documents of Catholic Social Teaching. Two of those are documents from Vatican II: *Gaudium et Spes* and *Dignitatis Humanae*. *Gaudium et Spes* speaks into some of the themes at the heart of Catholic Social Teaching—Life and Dignity of the Human Person; Family, Community and Participation; the Poor and Vulnerable; and the Dignity of Work and the Rights of Workers. *Dignitatis Humanae* speaks of the right to religious freedom based on the dignity of the human person. While it's important to note that Vatican II played such a key role in defining Catholic Social Teaching, we must recognize that Catholic social doctrine is comprised of thousands of years of tradition, history, and all the truths handed on to us by Christ Himself.

With her social teaching the Church seeks to proclaim the Gospel and make it present in the complex network of social relations. It is not simply a matter of reaching out to man in society — man as the recipient of the proclamation of the Gospel — but of enriching and permeating society itself with the Gospel. For the Church, therefore, tending to the needs of man means that she also involves society in her missionary and salvific work. The way people live together in society often determines the quality of life and therefore the conditions in which every man and woman understand themselves and make decisions concerning themselves and their vocation. For this reason, the Church is not indifferent to what is decided, brought about or experienced in society; she is attentive to the moral quality — that is, the authentically human and humanizing aspects — of social life. Society — and with it, politics, the economy, labor, law, culture — is not simply a secular and worldly reality, and therefore outside or foreign to the message and economy of salvation. Society in fact, with all that is accomplished within it, concerns man. Society is made up of men and women, who are 'the primary and fundamental way for the Church.'[43]

Living in the secular world, we see so many problems and things that need changing. We see a suffering society, a culture that doesn't know Christ. We see evil and sin running rampant. But, as we stated in prior chapters, there is great hope. And that hope begins with us. We *can* permeate society with the Gospel. We *can* tend to the needs of our fellow brothers and sisters. We *can* be attentive to the moral quality of social life. How? By diving into the beauty of Catholic Social Teaching and using it as our guide to accomplish all of these things and more.

There are eight principles of the Church's social doctrine, defined in the *Compendium of the Social Doctrine of the Church*. And while we will not solely focus on them, these principles are important to understand because they are the fundamental truths of Catholic social doctrine. They are:

- Meaning and Unity
- Participation
- The Fundamental Values of Social Life
- The Principle of Solidarity
- The Principle of Subsidiarity
- The Principle of the Common Good
- The Universal Destination of Goods
- The Way of Love

While all of these principles are worth diving into further because they directly relate to us as Catholic leaders, there are two that we'd like to more specifically discuss because of the versatility of their application to many areas of human activity: the principles of subsidiarity and solidarity.

Subsidiarity

Subsidiarity is the idea that decisions are better made at the local level.

The principle of subsidiarity protects people from abuses by higher-level social authority and calls on these same authorities to help individuals and intermediate groups to fulfill their duties...Experience shows that the denial of subsidiarity, or its limitation in the name of an alleged democratization or equality of all members of society, limits and sometimes even destroys the spirit of freedom and initiative.

In order for the principle of subsidiarity to be put into practice there is a corresponding need for: respect and effective promotion of the human person and the family.[44]

As lay Catholic leaders, we understand that true, virtuous leadership is being "someone who accomplishes great things by bringing out the greatness in others." The practice of subsidiarity is one of the many ways we can achieve virtuous leadership. Subsidiarity is the principle that all social bodies exist for the sake of the individual so that what individuals are able to do, society should not take over, and what small societies can do, larger societies should not take over.[45] Of course, this should be discussed in light of healthy politics and the way in which governments rule, but it can also be put into practice from where we stand as citizens of society. As the second paragraph of the quote above refers to, we must respect and promote every human person and the family, for that is who makes up communities, cities, states, countries, and the world. Practically speaking, the way we can live this out day-to-day is by employing solidarity in our lives, the second principle to be discussed.

Solidarity

Solidarity is...an authentic moral virtue...a 'firm and persevering determination to commit oneself to the *common good*. That is to say to the good of all and of each individual, because we are *all* really responsible *for all.*' Solidarity rises to the rank of fundamental *social virtue* since it places itself in the sphere of justice. It is a virtue directed *par excellence* to the *common good*, and is found in 'a commitment to the good of one's neighbor with the readiness, in the Gospel sense, to 'lose oneself' for the sake of the other instead of exploiting him, and to 'serve him' instead of oppressing him for one's own advantage.' (cf. *Mt* 10:40-42, 20:25; *Mk* 10:42-45; *Lk* 22:25-27).[46]

How we live out solidarity may vary from person-to-person. There are many ideas, responsibilities and interests to unite over. But what we can all understand about solidarity as a fundamental truth of Catholic social doctrine is that it is the moral virtue of committing ourselves to the common good of all. The common good, defined by the *Catechism of the Catholic Church*, is "the sum total of social conditions which allow people, either as groups or as individuals, to reach their fulfillment more fully and more easily."[47]

That is what Catholic Social Teaching and doctrine seek to achieve—the common good of all. Unfortunately, civil society often has a different idea of what the common good is than what the Church teaches. Thankfully, we have a guide, based on Truth, which we can turn to as we seek to live our Faith in the modern world.

We've barely scratched the surface of Catholic Social Teaching in this chapter, but our main goal is to give you a glimpse into this important element of formation for becoming a Catholic leader in civil society. We'd encourage and invite you to further explore the documents of the Church on this topic, as they are helpful in defining and clarifying the ways that we can morally live in this secular world and make the important and difficult decisions we must make as leaders. In the Appendix, you can find some of the writings we recommend. As you continue to pursue life as a Catholic leader, it is our hope and prayer that you will turn to the guidance of the Church first and foremost. There is so much our Catholic Faith has to offer.

Chapter 9
Six Fields for Civic Leadership

As the flames of your first enthusiasm die down, it becomes difficult to advance in the dark. —But that progress is all the more reliable for being hard. And then, when you least expect it, the darkness vanishes, and the enthusiasm and light return. Persevere![48]

Now that we've seen what the fundamentals for Catholic leadership in civil society are, let's discuss some practical applications of these fundamentals. We will now provide an overview of six key areas where lay Catholic leaders can be effective at influencing the world for Christ. These are: education, health care, immigration, business, news media, and religious liberty. The preceding is not an exhaustive list of fields that are ripe for the intervention of Catholic civic leaders, they are simply six areas that seem to be at the forefront of the cultural battles today. In each of these areas there are issues of concern to the Church. These are issues in which Catholic leaders in the secular world can exert a particular influence as leaders to advance the mission of the Church. We will examine each area and highlight some of their problems as they relate to civil society. It is our intention to provide some suggestions as to how lay Catholic leaders can step up and meet the needs or fill the gaps identified in each of these fields.

An ideology-infested education

Unfortunately, our own Catholic schools are not entirely unaffected by the expanding set of ideologies, which have made their way into the American education system. The problem, however, is much more accentuated in public schools, particularly in some states like California, where many of the curriculums in question originate. We say ideologies because there is certainly more than one ideology making its way through the textbooks, classes and culture in American schools. Many of these ideologies have found their genesis in Marxism and are anti-family, anti-freedom, and against religious-liberty: essentially anti-Catholic. Some examples of these are 'critical race theory,' which places all of American history within the framework of racism, and 'radical feminism,' which in seeking to elevate the value of women denies the complementarity of the sexes and the particular genius of each. Each manipulates history and distorts the Truth to advance an ideology or political agenda.

While there are many reasons to be concerned about these ideologies being taught primarily in the American public school system, by far the most troubling of them is gender ideology, which denies biology and the intrinsic value of our bodies. In public schools, gender ideology enters via a curriculum which is meant to promote same-sex marriage and so-called "transgender rights." Gender ideology is typically bundled up into courses and textbooks that also promote promiscuity, contraceptives, premarital sex and abortion in the public school system, all under the disguise of Comprehensive Sexuality Education (CSE). About CSE, the American College of Pediatricians has stated, "Less explicit, but included in CSE ideology, is the idea that young people should be free from sexual inhibitions, outdated moral constraints, and that adolescents should make up their own minds about when they are ready for sexual relations; adolescents should be free to enjoy sexual pleasure."[49]

The International Planned Parenthood Federation (IPPF), the international arm of Planned Parenthood, is one of the largest proponents of gender ideology and CSE around the world. Both organizations are the intellectual authors of many of the materials that make their way into American classrooms. IPPF has stated in one of its documents, "Young people (regardless of age, ethnicity, or culture) have sexual needs that go beyond these topics, as well as desires, fantasies and dreams related to their sexuality. For them to achieve and maintain a healthy development, they need to be able to explore, experience and express their sexuality."[50] IPPF advocates to "Guarantee access to hormone treatment for transgender and intersex adolescents."[51] They also ask for the removal of "A blanket requirement to report any sexual activity below a certain age" because it "can have the effect of deterring adolescents below this age from accessing services."[52]

So what is the problem with gender ideology and CSE? Besides the fact that they are built on ideology and not science, they essentially sexualize children, teaching them to consent to sex and ultimately perversions that reduce human sexuality to mere pleasure, often at the risk of objectifying the other person. CSE is not intended to create morals or protect children, nor is it meant to assist children struggling with serious sexual issues. The behaviors CSE encourages fuels a multi-billion dollar business, connected to contraception, abortion, sex-reassignment procedures, etc. that evidence has demonstrated don't actually help the individuals it is purported to serve. But what can lay Catholic leaders do about it?

For these dangerous and immoral materials to find their way into the American school system as part of the curriculum, there first has to have been a series of decisions made at the local public school system level, and also at the state and federal levels. It is precisely in these committees and at these meetings where disastrous decisions were made that we need more well-formed, faithful and committed Catholic voices. In fact, one should ask: where were the Catholics when these decisions were made decades ago? Demographics tell us that Catholics were probably present at those tables. The fact is that they either a) lacked Catholic formation and a proper understanding of the dignity of the human person, or b) they were not courageous enough to defend the children that would be affected by the proposed curriculum. We can't undo the harm these decisions caused overnight. It will take a long and hard struggle to bring some sanity back to our public schools' curriculum, but if we are to reverse the course, we must have more lay Catholic leaders ready to engage civil society in the area of education, particularly through running for seats at our public school districts, and seeking to exert more influence at our state departments of education as well as state and federal legislatures.

A lack of humanity in health care

Another area of human activity that is ripe for Catholic leadership is health care. The phrase "First do no harm" is a part of the original Hippocratic oath that many doctors still take as they begin their medical practices. What takes place afterwards, however, is not always consistent with the oath. To illustrate, here is a litany of modern attacks on the dignity of human persons in the field of health care: abortion, assisted suicide, cloning, contraception, end-of-life decisions, embryo grading, embryonic stem cell research, embryo "reduction," frozen embryos, gender ideology, human trafficking, in-vitro fertilization, research on fetuses, selling eggs, sperm donation, embryonic stem cell therapies, sterilization, surrogate motherhood, three-parent embryos, transgender therapies/surgeries, vaccines developed from fetal tissue, etc.

Many of the threats to human dignity we have listed stem from contemporary culture, or a subculture faithful Catholics call the "culture of death." They are the result of a disordered understanding of love, particularly sexual love. Ironically, as Catholics we do not lack the resources, teaching or guidance of the Church for better understanding how to approach these threats to human dignity. Sacred Scripture as well as many Church documents, such as *Humanae Vitae* (1968), *Evangelium Vitae* (1995), *Dignitas Personae* (2008) and the *Ethical and Religious Directives for Catholic Health Care Services* (USCCB) offer clear direction in all of these areas. What is lacking? We need more faithful Catholic doctors, lawyers and activists willing to take the risk to act in defense of the dignity of human life.

In *Evangelium Vitae*, St. John Paul II tells us "We are facing an enormous and dramatic clash between good and evil, death and life, the *culture of death* and the *culture of life*."[53] Some of us might say, what does all this have to do with me? I am not taking part in any of these evils. Maybe so, but as Catholics we also are taught that there is such a thing as a sin by omission. And so, John Paul II reminds us in the same document, "...in the midst of this conflict: we are all involved and we all share in it, with the inescapable responsibility of choosing to be unconditionally pro-life."[54] Lay Catholic leaders can no longer stand on the sidewalk of indifference. There are real sidewalks outside abortion centers that need us there! Our beloved St. John Paul II explained "...cultural transformation consists in forming consciences with regard to the incomparable and inviolable worth of every human life."[55] Furthermore, he insisted, "There is no true freedom where life is not welcomed and loved."[56]

The indifference to immigrants' suffering

Immigration is perhaps the most misunderstood (or ignored) area of Church teaching, particularly in countries like the United States, but not exclusively here. The issue of immigration and the Church's teaching on immigration is primarily—as it is the case with most issues of concern to the Church—a matter of human dignity. America is a country founded by immigrants. Of the two of us co-authors, Erin is a mixture of different ethnicities, including Irish, Swedish, German, Lithuanian, Italian and Polish, most of which encompass the historical Catholic experience of the United States that started with European immigrants arriving at Ellis Island. The other of us, Cristofer, is a first-generation immigrant from Peru and now a citizen of the United States. The immigrant experience is close to Cristofer's heart.

Recently as the attendee to a prominent conference of Catholic leaders in the United States, I (Cristofer) was saddened to see that a room that was previously filled with Catholics wanting to hear from a panel of bishops on the topic of the Latin Mass was almost emptied once the discussion ended and a new topic was introduced: immigration. Most of the people who left the room were Anglo Catholics. Was this a case of discrimination? We don't think so. Instead, there seems to be a misperception that the Catholic Church in the United States is advocating for an open-borders policy when it comes to immigration. This misreading of the Church's teaching on immigration causes some Catholics to want nothing to do with it.

While individual bishops might at times manifest their individual opinions when it comes to the matter at hand, the truth is the universal Church, through the Magisterium, as well as the United States Conference of Catholic Bishops, have always advocated for a merciful and caring treatment of immigrants. Jesus Himself was an immigrant, and the Holy Family experienced traveling to a new land where they would have been strangers trying to navigate a new culture. As it is always the case, the Catholic Church does not prescribe policy. Instead, it presents a set of principles to guide the laity as they drive or participate in the legislative processes of a nation. A policy of care and mercifulness cannot ever treat human beings as less than human. It also must first seek the unification and preservation of the family unit. The recipe for a just, humane, orderly, and common-sense immigration system is one that preserves the sovereignty of our nation and protects its borders simultaneously. It is up to us, the laity, to figure out how to achieve this. This is an area in urgent need of faithful Catholic voices at the table. But a first step must be to educate ourselves in the teaching of the Church with regards to immigration.

The vocation of the business leader

In 2014, the Pontifical Council for Justice and Peace at the Vatican published a document, which—like many of the virtually undiscovered treasures of the Church—has yet to find its way into the hands of most of its intended audience. It's called *Vocation of the Business Leader*. As the document itself explains, it "offers business leaders, members of their institutions, and various stakeholders a set of *practical principles* that can guide them in their service of the common good."[57]

There are many areas of the business world and market economy that the document touches on. Among them are the importance of developing businesses capable of supplying what human society really needs. Along with that, the Church invites business leaders to produce goods that are authentically placed at the service of humanity. The document makes an expressed invitation for business leaders to practice solidarity, especially with vulnerable populations and those in extreme need. *Vocation of the Business Leader* is also a call for the respect of human dignity and the dignity of human work. A staple of Catholic social doctrine, subsidiarity, is also mentioned by the document. There is a reference to the fact that subsidiarity is not only good for society but ultimately for a business itself. Lastly, the Church calls for "the sustainable creation of wealth," along with a responsible harnessing of resources.

Not of a Catholic origin, but surprisingly in line with Catholic social doctrine in many respects, and worth noting, is also the growing movement known as Conscious Capitalism. There have been many books written about it. The term itself has been trademarked by its strongest proponents. Some talk of it as a movement and there are several global corporations whose leadership align with its four basic pillars: purpose, stakeholder, culture and leadership. The ultimate consideration proposed by Conscious Capitalism is that a business which takes care of all of its stakeholders—employees, vendors, and clients included—is not only good for society but thrives because of this approach. Again, not flawless, nor initiated by Catholics, but Conscious Capitalism is in notable alignment with Catholic teaching and offers business leaders concrete steps in the right direction.

We invite those of you who are or aim to become business leaders to invest in a careful study of the principles proposed by the Catholic Church in *Vocation of the Business Leader*, and examine the progress made by initiatives, such as Conscious Capitalism, to advance the common good by making the world of business a fruitful field for Catholic leadership in civil society.

The Age of Fake Media

The hold of fake media on many contemporary information platforms predates the Trump era. Perhaps for a while many did not recognize its presence in society. Perhaps it was too well-disguised as real journalism. The fact is that the news media today is virtually unrecognizable from what it was two or three decades ago. It seems as though journalists are being trained to be *advocates*, not journalists. One of us co-authors—Cristofer—was a journalist who left television news in 2003. Back then, our job consisted of delivering information that was urgent, important and relevant. We would do this in an intelligible manner. We would try to present the facts through stories, but our job was never to convey our opinion. This was Journalism 101: you don't use characterizations or adjectives that convey your feelings towards a news story or its protagonists. We left that up to the audience.

Today the *Oxford* dictionary defines "fake news" as "false reports of events, written and read on websites."[58] In this age of social media, people's news is curated by algorithms that ultimately benefit from keeping us agitated and glued to our news feeds. However, it is widely understood that the reach of fake news goes beyond websites or social media. In fact, the most worrisome aspect of the current state of affairs in the news media is that fake news can be almost indistinguishable from real news. And yes, it can be and is often delivered by mainstream news outlets.

Does this mean that Catholics should simply give up on news media outlets? Should we stop consuming news content? Both of those ideas are simply unrealistic. Even for those who may have the least interest in news, there will always be a time when they need to be updated on recent events. Having accurate information serves the common good. For some the need is daily, for others it might be weekly, but our society functions better when everyone has at least a general grasp on what is going on around us. What we need is better journalism! The news media is a field that has been badly infected by the virus of fake news. This is also an arena in need of more lay Catholic leaders willing to invest in and create new and better news outlets. We need more Catholic leaders to join journalist guilds or associations. There need to be more books, conferences and initiatives created to promote an impartial and balanced approach to reporting the news. Universities need to form authentic journalists. Catholics in academia and in the newsroom have a responsibility to bring the Truth to the news.

The Fight for Religious Freedom

There are several ailments affecting every level of government in the United States today. Corruption, wasteful spending, lack of accountability, and inefficiency are some of the most common problems. Over the past few decades, the government—particularly at the federal and state levels—has slowly turned against the citizens it governs. We've seen this play out in three main areas: freedom of speech, freedom of conscience, and freedom of religion.

Just within the wedding industry, alone, there are numerous examples of legal cases brought against Christian artists who refused to use their talents on the celebration of so-called marriages because doing so would go against those artists' consciences and strongly held religious beliefs. We have seen the notorious case of Jack Phillips and his Masterpiece Cakeshop. There was also the case of Barronelle Stutzman from Arlene's Flowers, and finally Brush & Nib Studio, which creates wedding invitations, incorporating calligraphy and painting. In each of these cases, the business owners recognized the dignity of the individual and offered other services, but would not commit their personal creative talent to the celebration. There is a trend that manifests itself in government-initiated or -condoned legal harassment against individuals, private and nonprofit institutions, and those who will not embrace or promote contemporary society's ever-changing views on sexuality on the basis of religious beliefs.

In all three of the cases mentioned above, the refusal of a person's talents to celebrate a homosexual union was met with state-sanctioned harassment and, in extreme cases, the closing of their business. In the case of Masterpiece Cakeshop, a judge found that the city directly harassed Jack Phillips, going far beyond its mandate by using a religious litmus test to prevent him from operating his business. One more example of this is the case of New Hope Family Services. New York State's Office of Children and Family Services threatened to force this faith-based adoption provider to phase out of its adoption program simply because this nonprofit prioritized the placement of children into families with a married mother and father. All of these cases beg really important questions about religious freedoms, and exercising our conscience. For faithful Catholics, standing firm in the truth of our Faith when conducting business is important. Customers have the freedom to take their business anywhere! But to ask faithful Christians to defy their religious beliefs and conform to their customers' consciences impedes on our freedom of speech, freedom of conscience, and freedom of religion.

All of the cases mentioned above have the common denominator of having been defended in court by a noble organization to which we owe our admiration. Alliance Defending Freedom was co-founded by a Catholic man by the name of Alan Sears. Alan is a true example of what we are calling for in civil society. We need more Catholic legal teams and lawyers willing and able to protect religious freedom, free speech, marriage and family, parental rights, and the sanctity of life.

But that's not where the need ends. Our country is also crying out for faithful and committed Catholic men and women willing to step into the public square in order to serve their communities at every level of government. The need is great in our federal and state legislatures, and not a bit less urgent at lower levels of government, such as municipalities and public school districts. This, ladies and gentlemen, is where we really need the legions of Catholic men and women who had an experience of encounter or re-encounter with Christ. They might have just completed a Cursillo weekend, gone on a life-changing pilgrimage, or perhaps have recently endured a great loss, to the effect of wanting to seek God and bring their Catholic Faith alive. They are looking for their place in the Church and are ready to go on mission. It cannot be overstated: 1) We must go to the Church for community, to be revitalized by the sacraments and continue to grow in the Faith and our relationship with Christ. 2) However, our primary field for mission must be the secular world! This is our vocation. This is where the laity is urgently needed.

Chapter 10
Civic Leadership in Action

Be daring in your prayer, and the Lord will turn you from a pessimist into an optimist; from being timid, to being daring, from being feeble-spirited to being a man of faith, an apostle![59]

What does Catholic leadership in civil society *actually* look like? This chapter will provide clear examples and stories of known and not-so-well-known Catholic leaders in several areas of human activity and society. We've shared *a lot* of information with you, and we believe that it's also important to share exactly how to apply all of this information so that you can step into your role as a Catholic leader. God has called you to do something. May the examples we share in this chapter be an inspiration for you to answer that call!

We are blessed to have so many illustrations of faithful Catholics who've gone before us and who live amongst us today. They remind us that we are not alone in this journey to heaven, and they serve as a guide for us to be devoted followers of Christ in all that we do.

We've identified five Catholic leaders in different areas of human activity who we believe have truly benefited society and the Church: Tim Busch (business), St. Gianna Beretta Molla (healthcare/medicine), Dr. Andrew Abela (education), Amy Coney Barrett (government), and Jim Caviezel (media). As you read about each of these Catholic professionals, ask the Holy Spirit for the courage and grace you need to live your Faith boldly as they have.

Tim Busch — Founder of The Busch Firm and the Napa Institute, businessman, philanthropist, activist

Tim Busch is someone you may have heard of, who is a great Catholic leader in society. Busch has a robust résumé, but what makes him stand out the most is how he lives his Catholic Faith outwardly. As a businessman in secular and faith-based atmospheres, he handles his affairs keeping Christ at the forefront.

Perhaps Tim's most notable Catholic leadership is his work at the Napa Institute, which he founded "in an effort to train Catholic leaders to defend the Faith in an increasingly secular society."[60] However, his leadership in civil society extends far beyond this. Busch is considered one of the most influential laymen in the United States, as he is involved in a multitude of Catholic entities: The Magis Institute, EWTN, and Legatus, just to name a few. Busch receives much of his spiritual direction from Opus Dei priests and the *Catechism of the Catholic Church*, both amazing sources for the truth of our Faith.[61]

Busch's Catholic leadership clearly benefits the Church, but how does it benefit society? As a business leader, Busch's influence reaches far beyond our Church. For example, Tim is a proponent of and often talks about a fair wage. Guided by Catholic Social Teaching, he has stated, "You can't be a good Catholic and pay wages which are not adequate to live on."[62] Of course his employees probably appreciate this, but more than that, he is setting an example for the business community. Wages affect everyone, and adequate wages are important. It is not surprising that Tim is one of the forces behind the annual Principled Entrepreneurship Conference. These are just some examples of the many ways Tim benefits our society. We encourage you to read more about his influence in the Catholic community and beyond.

St. Gianna Beretta Molla — Pediatric physician, wife and mother

Many Catholics are familiar with St. Gianna Beretta Molla, who in less than 40 years, became a physician, wife, mother and saint! St. Gianna was canonized in 2004 and has been an inspiration to people across the world for the way she bravely lived her Faith.

Gianna was born in Italy. She earned degrees in medicine and surgery from the University of Pavia, eventually specializing in pediatrics. She was also an active member of the Society of St. Vincent de Paul and a leader in the Catholic Action movement. In 1952, Gianna opened a clinic in the town of Mesero, where she met Pietro Molla, whom she married in 1955. In the next four years the Mollas had three children. Two pregnancies following ended in miscarriage.[63]

Early in her final pregnancy, doctors discovered that Gianna had both a child and a tumor in her uterus. She allowed the surgeons to remove the tumor but not to perform the complete hysterectomy that they recommended, which would have killed the child. Seven months later in April 1962, Gianna Emanuela Molla was born, but postoperative complications resulted in an infection for her mother. The following week, Gianna Beretta Molla died at home.[64]

St. Gianna's Catholic leadership was intertwined into her daily life as a doctor, wife and mother. Her life story is also a story of profound Catholic leadership in civil society. Her marriage, motherhood, and career were all ordered toward and reflections of her Faith. Two things we want to point out specifically are the way she lived her marriage and the way she practiced her work as a pediatric physician. Before their marriage, Gianna wrote to Pietro, "Love is the most beautiful sentiment that the Lord has put into the soul of men and women."[65] This and so much more can be found in *The Journey of Our Love: The Letters of Saint Gianna Beretta and Pietro Molla*. It contains the letters between Gianna and Pietro throughout their marriage, which reflect the daily experiences, the abundant love of, and true holiness lived by a modern-day couple. In her work as a doctor, Gianna abided by the teachings of the Catholic Church, truly upholding the dignity of the human person in everything she did.

St. Gianna's Catholic leadership benefited society and the Church back then and it continues to benefit both now. Giving her life so that her daughter may live, she became a perfect model of Christ's love in a situation that was both medical and spiritual. Women of all faiths and walks of life experience childbirth and motherhood, and most (we hope all) would do *anything* for their children. St. Gianna's example is one that men and women everywhere can look to for strength, hope, and love in the most important moment of their lives, as they discern all the decisions they will have to make as they bring new life into the world.

Dr. Andrew Abela — Dean and Ordinary Professor of Marketing in the Busch School of Business at the Catholic University of America

Dr. Andrew Abela is another great example of a Catholic leader in civil society. As the founding dean of the Busch School of Business and Ordinary Professor of Marketing at The Catholic University of America, in Washington, D.C., Dr. Abela has contributed much in research on the integrity of the marketing process, including marketing ethics, Catholic Social Doctrine, and internal communication. In addition to being published in several academic journals, he co-edited *A Catechism for Business*, and was awarded for that work by the Acton Institute for "significant contributions to the study of the relationship between religion and economic liberty."[66]

Although "Professor" and "Dean" are the titles he's most known for, we would like to focus on Dr. Abela's writings, which have reached far beyond his classroom and have affected the minds and hearts of Catholics everywhere. He is the author of numerous business articles, including—"The Economic Message of 'Evangelii Gaudium,'" "Protecting Life at Work," "Workplace Responsibilities," "Life in the Balance," and "A Catechism for Business." Because of his writings, Dr. Abela is referred to as "a champion of Catholic business ethics."[67] He believes that ethics and their relationship to Catholicism is clear. Additionally, *A Catechism for Business: Tough Ethical Questions & Insights from Catholic Teaching*, the book that Abela co-edited, makes Church teaching accessible so that business people can act ethically in business situations. The book both asks and answers tough questions and illustrates the link between morality and a strong economy.[68]

Dr. Andrew Abela's Catholic leadership in civil society is obvious. His roles as dean and professor, writer and marketing expert are each a reflection of his Catholic Faith. We need people like this in our society, who permeate their work with their Catholic worldview. His leadership benefits society through the young minds he educates at Catholic University of America, and in his work outside of the classroom as a writer, marketing expert, consultant and trainer. He is greatly benefiting our Church through his work, inspiring the minds and hearts of Catholics everywhere and educating them on worldly things with a Catholic lens.

Amy Coney Barrett — Associate Justice of the Supreme Court of the United States

Amy Coney Barrett was quickly propelled into the public eye in 2020 when President Trump nominated her to a seat vacated by Ruth Bader Ginsburg, who passed away. Barrett was confirmed by the Senate and received commission on October 26, 2020. Amy Coney Barrett is a Catholic, a mother of seven, and pro-life. In the time leading up to her confirmation and commission, Barrett gracefully navigated a media industry that was using lies to sway the public's reputation of her: harsh political jargon, threats to her family, and a brutal attack on her Catholic Faith. In the midst of it all, she stood resolute in her commitment to God, her family, and the good of this country. Three distinct examples of Barrett's Catholic leadership are the following: (1) her opening statement at her confirmation hearing, (2) her response in an interview at Hillsdale College about her Faith and (3) that she was unaffected by a comment made in her confirmation to the Seventh Circuit Court in 2017 that directly attacked her Faith and came up again in 2020 when she was nominated to the Supreme Court.

Barrett's opening statement at her confirmation hearing was this: "I believe in the power of prayer and it has been uplifting to hear that so many people are praying for me."[69] Through these words and actions and others in this hearing, she illustrated beautifully what it means to be unashamed of our Catholic beliefs in the public square.

In an interview at Hillsdale College, Barrett said: "We have a long tradition of religious tolerance in this country, and in fact the 'religious test' clause in the Constitution makes it unconstitutional to impose a religious test on anyone who holds public office. So whether someone is…Catholic or Jewish or Evangelical or Muslim or has no faith at all is irrelevant to the job, and, in fact, it's unconstitutional to consider it as a qualification for office. When you step back and you think about the debate about whether someone's religion has any bearing on their fitness for office, it seems to me that the premise of the question is that people of faith would have a uniquely difficult time separating out their moral commitments from their obligation to apply the law. And I think people of faith should reject that premise."[70]

In 2017, when Senator Dianne Feinstein questioned Barrett for her confirmation to the Seventh Circuit Court, she went so far as to warn that "the dogma" of the Catholic Faith "lives loudly" in Barrett, and that this was "of concern," despite the fact that Article 6 of the United States Constitution states that "no religious test shall ever be required as a qualification to any office or public trust under the United States." In 2020, when Barrett was under attack by the press, Catholics everywhere took it upon themselves to make a statement out of this quote and proudly wear, share and promote it as a very good thing and something that we are not afraid of, that is not at all "of concern." "The dogma lives loudly within me" became a phrase that was printed on shirts, posters, cards, coffee mugs, etc.— items that sold out almost immediately.

Amy Coney Barrett's Catholic leadership has benefited the Church by bringing into the light what it looks like to be a Catholic figure who adheres to the Church's teachings in one of the harshest areas of human activity—the law. She benefits society by using her morals and Catholic worldview to make decisions on the biggest issues at hand in our country.

We must note that there is a distinction between political figures who are Catholic but do not practice or adhere to the Church's teachings and those who are practicing Catholics and call on the Church's teachings to inform and guide how they govern and/or lead. Barrett is an example of the latter, which is why we've shared her as an example of a Catholic leader.

Jim Caviezel — Actor

Everyone knows Jim Caviezel as the actor who portrayed Jesus Christ in *The Passion of the Christ*. But what's amazing about Caviezel is that his Faith is not just something he "acts" on the screen. He fully embraces his Catholic Faith off-screen, very boldly and intensely. He is particularly well-spoken *and outspoken* about the Catholic Faith when he's interviewed and in front of an audience. His boldness is a true testament to St. John Paul II's statement "Be not afraid!" that rings out in many of our Catholic communities today. Caviezel starred in the 2019 film *Infidel*, and in 2020 he was featured in several interviews regarding the film and its message. One interview in particular stands out. Caviezel chose to use this as an opportunity to speak the Truth to the people interviewing him and to the viewers about what he saw happening in the United States in 2020. He proudly lives and believes in Jesus Christ and the Catholic Church. It's beautiful to see someone in the spotlight sharing so boldly.

During a *Fox and Friends Weekend* interview on September 19, 2020, Caviezel said of the film *Infidel*: "The goal is to bring attention to a lot of Americans about the persecution that's going on in Iran...countries like China...Christian persecution where they execute them for their Faith. People have taken their Faith for granted, especially here in the United States. Now, with not being able to go to churches, which is a violation of our inalienable rights, we need to start standing up."[71]

The interviewer asked him, "Why are Christians not standing up?" to which Caviezel replied: "...the fear factor. But Jesus says, 'Do not be afraid. I go before you always.'"[72]

And on his roles in *The Passion of the Christ* and *Infidel*, Caviezel shared that he approached them "...with the intention to bring souls back to Jesus."[73]

Jim Caviezel's examples of leadership are much more intense than the previous ones we've shared. It is good for us to see a wide range of perspectives and approaches to living as Catholic leaders because everyone's style is different. Regardless of "style," the most important parts of being a Catholic leader in civil society are an adherence to the Catholic Church's teachings, living with integrity and approaching one's role with love and selflessness. Caviezel certainly does these things, but with a passionate conviction that we don't often see. His Catholic leadership benefits society and the Church as he portrays for us what it means to be a Christian, even in the midst of persecution, on and off screen.

Hopefully these examples have given you a better understanding of what exactly Catholic leadership in civil society looks like, how it starts, and how it benefits society and the Church. Notice how each person mentioned above witnesses their Faith in a way that is unique to who they are and the gifts they have been given. You may not be called to be an award winning actor or a Supreme Court justice, but you are called to bring your Faith into every aspect of your life. You can pursue whatever the Lord is calling you to! As you can see, you can do this in whatever season of life or whatever vocation you are in.

Can you identify at least one aspect of the leadership we've illustrated in this chapter that you can apply to your own life? Perhaps Tim Busch's philanthropic heart or St. Gianna's adherence to the Truth in trials. Perhaps Dr. Abela's education through a Catholic worldview or Amy Coney Barrett's and Jim Caviezel's boldness. We challenge you to take the first step in implementing it this week!

Chapter 11
Board Service, Where Leadership Happens

Mediocre men, mediocre in mind and in Christian spirit, surround themselves by foolish people when they are in power. They are falsely persuaded by their vanity that in this way they will never lose control.

Sensible men, however, surround themselves with learned people who live a clean life as well as possessing knowledge, and become, through their help, men who can really govern. They are not in this matter deceived by their humility, for in making others great they themselves are made great.[74]

So far, we've shared with you the stories of past and current lay Catholic leaders. We've also discussed specific areas where Catholic leadership for civil society can be carried out. But we've left the best for last! There is one area that research, careful analysis, and meticulous observation of contemporary society has identified as the ultimate field for civic leadership. Why? Because of its potential to impact society and the fact that it is uniquely all-encompassing. It impacts every organization, and every area of enterprise. This is board service. Keep in mind that for our purposes, and our urgent call to action, we have broadened the definition of "board service."

By "board service," we are certainly referring to real and actual boards of organizations. We are referring to for-profit, nonprofit, governmental or private, boards of directors, advisory boards, and fundraising boards. But we are also referring to governmental bodies that legislate or dictate ordinances or policies. And not only these, we are pushing the boundaries of the definition of board service to also include committees, subcommittees, campaign cabinets, and councils of every kind. There is more. We want to include here student government bodies at universities, Rotary Clubs, Lions Clubs, homeowners associations, parent-teacher associations—in other words, all of the tables where decisions are made in the secular world!

All of the inhumane and often destructive decisions being made by contemporary society—the decisions that are hurting the world we inhabit and negatively impacting the culture—are being made by a group, large or small, of people sitting around a (now sometimes virtual) table. What we have come to understand is that board service (in the very broad sense we just defined) is where leadership happens! Not that we would characterize decisions which are damaging to society as "leadership." They are not. But the same place and in the same manner in which these unfortunate and misguided decisions are made is the place where well-formed, faithful and committed Catholic leaders can make a difference by changing the direction society is headed towards. Many who serve on boards find that often bad decisions are not made by bad people, but by those who are confused and need to be challenged by our witness.

If board service is new to you, we invite you to learn more about it and engage society through it. Just to get you started, we will briefly examine some of the different aspects of board service, as well as the types of board service there are. Additionally, we'll highlight some of the concrete opportunities available to Catholic leaders in civil society through board service.

Why serve on a board?

To those with board experience the answer might be obvious, but to the audience we intend to reach—Catholic professionals who might not have considered or had an opportunity to participate in board service—a response is in order. When a Catholic leads in civil society through board service, everyone wins. This includes the Church, the community, the organization being served, and the board member, as well. Having more lay Catholic professionals who are well-formed, faithful, and committed to their Catholic Faith, sitting at a table where decisions are made can only bring about good to society. You, the Catholic board members, are the voice of the Church! You are the Church's ambassadors, advocates, and champions, serving not only the Church, but the common good. This is a function of enormous importance and implication to society and the work of the Church. These are roles that in most instances simply cannot be occupied by the clergy. The benefits of bringing Catholic social doctrine, a regard for the protection of human dignity, and a sense of integrity to the tables where decisions are made can bring about the change we pray for in society! The Church benefits through the creation of a fertile ground in which our pastors can deliver the message of the Gospel without opposition. The community benefits from morally sound decisions. The organization being served can only benefit from being oriented towards the common good by the influence of a board member who possesses a Christian worldview. Ultimately, as God can never be outdone in generosity, the Catholic board member personally benefits in terms of networking, career growth and access to collaborations and professional opportunities that can only come about as a result of active board service.

How else does board service benefit the Church and the common good?

Let us go back now and think, one by one, of the examples we offered before in our broad (re)definition of board service. In the case of a for-profit (private or public) corporation whose board is made up of one or more Catholic leaders, the enterprise will benefit from the influence of one or a group of people in the business world who have an understanding of the vocation of a business leader. It goes back to a care for each of the stakeholders in a corporation, not just its stockholders. The potential for impact in the nonprofit world is just as large. The nonprofit world consists of tons of different sectors, such as health care and education, but also made out of organizations that seek to meet basic and immediate needs. For example, the mission of St. Vincent de Paul is to "feed, clothe, house, and heal." But it does not necessarily have to be a Catholic nonprofit for Catholic leaders to have an impact in civil society. The range of areas of human activity where a lay Catholic leader can have an impact is also extensive in any legislative role or level of government. These also constitute a type of board where well-formed faithful and committed Catholics are needed. Simply thinking of the many pro-life laws that have been passed by states like Arizona and Texas is inspiring. Earlier, we also talked about the potential for impact a lay Catholic leader can have taking a seat on a public school board. The possibilities simply are endless.

Duties and Challenges

Board membership of course comes with duties and challenges. But every Catholic professional equipped with a well-formed conscience and solid understanding of Catholic social doctrine and the dignity of the human person should be up to the challenge. There are three primary duties of a board member toward the organization being served that are in parallel with some of our duties as Catholics towards our beloved Catholic Faith. These are the duty to care, the duty of loyalty, and the duty of obedience.

The three should be somewhat self-explanatory, but we will expand on the specifics as board service unfolds in real life. A board member must demonstrate their care of the organization by making an attempt to attend meetings and be prepared to participate in constructive ways. They should also, when possible, attend special events and represent the board. A board member should be loyal and act as an advocate for the organization. A board member should always keep up-to-date on developments in the organization and the organization's field of action. From time to time, a board member will be asked to serve on committees or special task forces. Out of a just obedience to their role it is the duty of each board member to be knowledgeable of the board's policies and by-laws as well as the organization's services, policies, and programs. In most instances, board members need to actively support the organization financially, as well, and/or solicit donors on their behalf.

So, what are the challenges in board service? These can be grouped into three distinct types: the people, the issues and the commitment. The people around the table in a boardroom can become the greatest strength and dynamism of an organization, but at times, through a culture of dysfunctionality, they can also become the demise of the organization they are called to serve. Also, the issues that an organization and its board will face will vary largely depending on its identity and mission, the organization's financial health, and ethical (or lack thereof) practices. A board is supposed to guide the organization towards its goals and objectives. In other words, a board is to help the organization fulfill its mission and protect its identity. This is why the board exists. The commitment to board service can certainly become a great challenge when the time, talent or treasure required of the board member is not in line with their availability, capacity or means. This is why expectations must be clear from the beginning when entering board service.

Types of boards

There are primarily two types of boards that a Catholic leader in civil society can be involved in, with the addition of a third type that sometimes can be exclusive or merged into the first two. The primary two types of boards are governing and advisory boards. The third type is the fundraising board, which often comes into play as part of the first two, but at times exists as a body of its own. The board of directors for an organization is the ultimate authority over it. It is where the final and most important decisions are made. Even the organization's director, president or CEO (who may or may not have a seat on the board) is subordinate to the board as a whole. A governance board, often called a board of directors, and its members, can be very powerful. The other type of board, the advisory board, does primarily what its name implies. It is typically made up of experts, people with a certain knowledge that is needed by the organization. Their influence in the decision-making process is very important, but not ultimate. However, opportunities to serve on the advisory boards of key organizations should not be passed on by Catholic leaders. There is much that can be accomplished for the common good from an advisory board. These board positions often lead to a seat in an organization's board of directors. Fundraising boards can exist simply to fundraise, and, because of their purpose, their impact can be large and very significant for the organization. Very often, members of a governance and even advisory board would have a fundraising duty. Sometimes this is a fixed annual amount that the board member must personally give or raise from others.

As mentioned before, committees and subcommittees—which are created with an action item or specific purpose in sight—are sort of advisory boards in practice. They typically do not have ultimate decision-making authority, but they can have a certain level of authority within the scope of their mission. They can also be very influential in an organization. The same can be said of councils or cabinets. The different types of civic clubs that exist, homeowners associations and parent-teacher associations can take on different roles, forms, duties, decision-making capacities, goals and objectives. A Catholic leader will always find governance, advisory and/or fundraising models at the heart of most of these boards. They are all wonderful opportunities to influence society for Christ, influencing our secular institutions with the values of the Gospel.

Chapter 12
Excellence and Relationships

Don't despise little things, for by the continual practice of denying yourself again and again in such things — which are never futile or trivial — with God's grace you will add strength and resilience to your character. In that way you will first become master of yourself, and then a guide, a chief, a leader: to compel and to urge and to inspire others, with your word, with your example, with your knowledge and with your power.[75]

As Catholic professionals and leaders, we are called to glorify God and "be the light" in all we do. Excellence and relationships are at the heart of this.

God created all things "to show forth and communicate his glory." [Cf. Vatican Council I, Dogm. Const. Dei Filius, canon 5] By making our work a participation in his creative power, he wanted it to reflect his glory. Let your light so shine before men, that they may see your good works and give glory to your Father who is in heaven. [Mt 5:16] The sanctification of our professional work requires that we carry it out as perfectly as possible, for love of God, so that it becomes a light that draws those around us to him.[76]

For our purposes, we will define "excellence" as "living a virtuous life to become like God; striving for holiness in everything; becoming a saint." In fact, in the Greek translation of the Bible, the word "arete," commonly used for "excellence," directly translates to "virtuous." Let us be clear that excellence is not the same as perfection. Perfection does not leave any room for humility; excellence does. That said, in the above excerpt from Opus Dei's "Professional Prestige" article, we'd encourage you to read the last sentence of the paragraph like this instead: "The sanctification of our professional work requires that we carry it out as *excellently* as possible..."

When we glorify God in all that we do, instead of seeking our own glory, we are exhibiting the kind of humility that true leadership requires. Some Catholics believe that Christian humility is in contradiction with professional ambition or aspirations to success. Nothing could be further from the truth. If a Catholic professional seeks to establish a good professional reputation and increased career success in a virtuous way, he or she is better able to support the mission of the Church. The key is for one's heart to remain in the right place — with Christ. Success for the sake of success is not of Christ, but if it becomes an instrument to bring others to Him, then it can become an effective means of evangelization.

> *This plan for the spiritual life of the laity should take its particular character from their married or family state or their single or widowed state, from their state of health, and from their professional and social activity. They should not cease to develop earnestly the qualities and talents bestowed on them in accord with these conditions of life, and they should make use of the gifts which they have received from the Holy Spirit.*
> *...They should also hold in high esteem professional skill, family and civic spirit, and the virtues relating to social customs, namely, honesty, justice, sincerity, kindness, and courage, without which no true Christian life can exist.*[77]

This excerpt from *Apostolicum Actuositatem* teaches us that excellence requires, first, an understanding of our vocation(s) and the activities that fill our time. Then, we can more properly develop our God-given qualities, talents and the gifts bestowed on us by the Holy Spirit in every part of our lives. It specifically names honesty, justice, sincerity, kindness, and courage as the virtues that define a truly Christian life. How blessed we are to have a roadmap for living an excellent life!

Our culture seems to have relaxed many things—manners, language and dress to name a few—and prioritized the wrong things—working all the time, complacency, and disregard for the dignity of others. Many things have become very casual and lax. The way of our language has gone the way of our culture. Constant work has replaced rest and holy leisure. Complacency, or being satisfied with how things are and not wanting to try to make them better, has replaced excellence. All of this is to the detriment of our dignity, excellence, and relationships! As Catholic professionals, it is our responsibility to raise the bar, set the standard higher, and call those around us to greatness as we exhibit greatness ourselves. We want to change the culture and the narrative of professionalism.

We've identified four practices that every Catholic professional should exhibit. We'll call them the "Four Practices of Excellence":

1. **Arrive on time**: Showing up on time is an act of charity. When we arrive early or on time to an event, meeting, or any planned encounter with others, we are respecting their dignity and their schedule. Your time is theirs until the event, meeting, etc. is over.
2. **A good handshake**: Greeting others with a firm handshake and making eye contact while doing so is the mark of a true professional. Not only is this a respectful practice, it affirms their dignity and expresses they are important to you. In some cultures, a bow is more ordinary than a handshake. It communicates the same thing, and doing it well is an important way to honor the other.
3. **Professional attire**: "A suit [, dress, blouse and skirt, etc.] is nothing but a garment, but when that [outfit] is worn by someone who has prepared him or herself professionally and taken on the life-long commitment of building a virtuous character, that [outfit] can be a conduit to great professional opportunities...a [professional] business [outfit]–when worn with intentionality–can be the laity's cassock or habit. We too can tell the world we mean business, God's business...when a Catholic lay person has formed him or herself, worked to develop a virtuous character and

received the adequate professional education, a [professional business outfit, such as a suit, dress, etc.] can be that person's entrance to a world of possibilities that, quite simply, a lack of professional appearance would otherwise deny."[78]

4. **Follow-up**: This is crucial! Whether it's an email, a card in the mail or a phone call, following up with others is a great habit. It gives you an opportunity to, most importantly, thank them for their time. It also allows you to leave your contact information/business card and say anything that you left unsaid while you were with them in-person. People appreciate being appreciated. Even if everything went fantastic while you were with them, you still want to follow up with *something*, however simple it may be.

In addition to the above, living an excellent professional life encompasses many other things, namely, various forms of etiquette—email, networking, business meals and board rooms. We'll first discuss email etiquette, as it is slightly different from the other three.

- **Email etiquette**: Emails are a part of every professional's life. For some, it is the main form of communication they use throughout their workday. Thus, it is very important that we practice strong email etiquette. Here's how:
    - Respond to emails within 24-48 hours.
    - Include a clear, direct subject line.
    - Use a professional email address, professional salutations and classic/standard fonts.
    - Keep a positive tone in your message, even if what you're writing isn't great news.
    - Sign every email with the same professional signature, one that includes your first and last name, title, company, and your contact information.
    - Proofread every message before pressing "Send."

The Four Practices of Excellence must already be included as part of the following three types of etiquette. So, in addition to those, here is what else must be considered in the following environments:

- **Networking etiquette**: Networking is when first impressions are made. It's been said that "you never get a second chance to make a good first impression." So these opportunities are key and must be capitalized on! In these situations, employing the following can help you land that good first impression every time:
    - Have a small stack of your business cards handy, so when the time comes, you aren't fumbling around in your purse, pockets, etc. to find them!
    - Come prepared with 2-3 questions you want to ask the person/people you will encounter to learn more about them and potential opportunities for collaboration.
    - Keep an open mind.
    - Go into each conversation with the intention to do more listening than talking.
    - Take notes about each person you meet during or after the event so you can have good follow-up later.
- **Business meal etiquette**: When people gather, it is most often around a meal. In the business setting, it's imperative that we practice proper etiquette during meals with other professionals. The casual culture we live in nowadays seems to have forgotten business meal etiquette. However, as Catholic professionals, let us put this etiquette into practice and live out excellence in this way!
    - The person doing the inviting is the host and leads the meal/experience (for example, he or she sits first and eats first).
    - It is best not to order alcohol during the meal (unless it's provided by the host).
    - Manners matter. Some basic manners to put into practice are:
        1) order something that is not difficult to eat,
        2) make sure your napkin is placed on your lap before you begin eating,
        3) chew with your mouth closed, and
        4) swallow your food before engaging in conversation.

- For a complete guide to business meal etiquette, please see the appendix for a document that we've identified as one of the best and most thorough manuals for successful business dining.
- **Boardroom etiquette**: Simple, difficult, and important decisions are made by boards. As a board member, you have a responsibility to yourself, the people in the room, and the organization to show respect and kindness in every situation and keep charity at the forefront of every interaction and discussion.
  - Participate in the discussion when you have something essential to contribute.
  - Speak when spoken to. If your input is not asked for, but you have something to say, speak when there is a pause in the conversation. Do not interrupt anyone while he or she is speaking.
  - Keep your area clean. If at a large conference table, have a notepad and pen (and your drink, if drinks have been provided) in front of you, but keep everything else off the table.
  - Make sure you know who is in the room and properly address each person by his or her correct title and name.

As you can see, the way of our excellence goes the way of our relationships. The more we live an honest, just, sincere, kind, and courageous life—an excellent life—what follows is a life that builds profound relationships with God, ourselves, and others. As we develop into virtuous professionals, so too, will our relationships develop, and for the better. We are meant to live in communion with one another. Instilling excellence—in all its forms—into our daily life, can lead us to that communion.

Excellence truly is about giving God all the glory. As Catholic leaders in civil society, it is our role to instill what we've discussed in this chapter as instruments to bring others to Christ, as effective means of evangelization. Excellence leads to great relationships. In other words, "Christian virtues enlivened by charity"[79] are what draw souls to God. May our humility, disposition of our hearts, professional ambitions, and successes enhance our relationships and support the mission of the Church by bringing others to Christ.

Chapter 13
Work as a Service to Others

We must be convinced therefore that work is a magnificent reality, and that it has been imposed on us as an inexorable law which, one way or another, binds everyone... It is an indispensable means which God has entrusted to us here on this earth. It is meant to fill out our days and make us sharers in God's creative power. It enables us to earn our living and, at the same time, to reap 'the fruits of eternal life'...[80]

Work as a service to others is one of the most important ways to live our Catholic leadership in civil society, and St. Josemaría Escrivá's words beautifully illustrate this. This statement challenges the common way many of us view our work. It is countercultural, yet, it is what we are invited to embrace and embody. We have been *entrusted* to take part in God's creativity and *reap the benefits of eternal life.* WOW! This completely defies the self-centered model of work geared toward one's own satisfaction and replaces it with the truth that our work is not only a service to God, but to His creation, our fellow man. There is a particular mindset we are called to have when approaching our work—a mindset that seeks to serve and uplift others. What is the benefit they will receive? How can I adapt my work to their needs? What is the best way I can serve? Finding and living the answers to these questions in our daily work can transform how we approach our jobs and allow us to have a *servant mindset,* a mindset focused on using our gifts and talents to serve and uplift others.

Laying the Foundation for a Mindset that Serves and Uplifts

Our work is meant to fulfill the vocation God has called us to, so much so that we work directly in union with Him and become who we are meant to be through it.

> *Be convinced that our professional vocation is an essential and inseparable part of our condition as Christians. Our Lord wants you to be holy in the place where you are, in the job you have chosen for whatever reason. To me, every job that is not opposed to the divine law is good and noble, and capable of being raised to the supernatural plane, that is, inserted into the constant flow of Love which defines the life of a child of God.*[81]

Before we can live with a servant mindset, we must have a strong foundation, described above by St. Josemaría: Work is a part of who we are, it makes us holy, and fulfills our lives as children of God (when it is not opposed to divine law).

The Importance

As mentioned earlier, we have been *entrusted* to take part in God's creativity, which means our work is a service *to God and to each other*. It may be difficult to understand the importance of this if you view your job as just a means to an end, if you dislike the work you do, or even if you take so much pride in your work that you see it as only possible because of you and not because of God working in you. Let us share an example of the importance of what we've been entrusted with. Say you work at an ice cream shop and perhaps you don't see this work as "fulfilling God's plan for your life." However, by scooping and serving ice cream with a smile on your face, cleaning the shop, washing dishes, keeping inventory, etc., you are taking part in God's creativity because without you doing these things, the business would not thrive, customers would be less happy, and people's lives would be negatively affected. By having a servant mindset even in this job, you are taking part in God's plan for you, the shop owner and the people you serve.

Living the Mindset

Now that we've laid the foundation and explained the importance of a servant mindset, how can someone actually live it? One of the best things to do is to ask ourselves at the start of each day, *How can I serve and uplift those whom I will encounter today?* We can use our answers to this and the following questions as a daily guide.

Think about a time when someone went out of his or her way to serve you and your life was made better because of it. How did you feel? What impression did it leave on you? Did this impact you in a way that caused you to change the way you serve your customers and clients?

A practical way to instill this in your life is to begin each day thinking through your planned encounters and writing out your responses to the questions posed above and more clearly defined below. It will put you in the right headspace, and who knows, you may just find your work is more fulfilling and life-giving!

- *How can I serve and uplift those whom I will encounter today?*
- *How did I feel when [name] went out of his/her way to serve me?*
- *What impression did this leave on me?*
- *How can I change how I serve my customers and clients so I can leave the same impression?*

...But Not at Your Own Expense

In discussing this topic, it is important to address that serving others in your work should not come at the expense of your joy, well-being and the ability to do your job. It's a great thing when you can take pride in your work and enjoy what you do. Serving others should complement that, not get in the way of it. A few simple ways to do this are as follows:

- **Set boundaries.** Work the hours you are paid to work and then turn off your notifications for the night. You are not

- at everyone's beck and call 24/7. Someone's needs for your services can wait until tomorrow.
- **You are allowed to say "no."** You do not have to say "yes" to everything and, in fact, you shouldn't if you want to be able to do your job well.
- **It is acceptable to disagree with someone.** You are not going to see eye-to-eye with everyone on everything, and, more importantly, you do not have to. Embrace that fact and learn to offer solutions or alternatives when disagreements arise.

It is possible to serve others, take care of yourself, and be proud of your work all at the same time. God will never give us more than we can handle, but He also doesn't ask us to do so many things for so many people that we neglect to take care of ourselves and relinquish our pride in our work.

Since we have been entrusted with taking part in God's divine plan for creation, He has big plans for the work we do! Having a servant mindset helps us approach our work as a way to benefit others and fulfill our vocations because when we love our neighbor as ourselves, seek to serve, and engage in moral work, we are made holy. With a strong foundation of Faith, an understanding of the importance of a servant mindset, and a balance of serving others while taking care of oneself, work as a service to others will transform our lives.

Chapter 14
Called to Be Faithful

Sanctity is made up of heroic acts. Therefore, in our work we are asked for the heroism of finishing properly the tasks committed to us, day after day, even though they are the same tasks. If we don't, then we do not want to be saints![82]

The complexities of the society we now inhabit and the contradicting forces at work within it continue to pin Catholics into different corners. Many lay Catholic professionals wonder where they should stand on the political or cultural spectrum in order to be true to their Faith. So how does a Catholic leader know if he or she is being faithful to the Magisterium and orthodox in the practice of the Faith, or simply being "brainwashed"?

We hope we have provided you with some answers to this question. However, this chapter will explore the "call to faithfulness" that has been placed in front of each one of us. We'll first focus on an example that perhaps you can relate to. Recently, a Catholic in our network who was offered—and later decided to pass on—an opportunity for leadership development, provided the following explanation over email (We have intentionally left it anonymous.):

"The more complicated part of the reason (to decline the offer) is that my wife was surprisingly unsupportive of my participation. Ultimately, she relented when I pressed the issue and said that I wanted to participate. I am sharing her concern because I think it speaks to the issue(s) this organization is trying to address. Her concern is that I would be "brainwashed" to be ultra-conservative. To her this means being anti-gay, anti-women, and, most of all, anti-compassion. She said that while we are practicing Catholics—these are not the "types of Catholics" that we are. While I was willing to continue in spite of her concerns, I have to admit that this did weigh into my decision."

This concerned Catholic's hesitation and ultimate decision not to participate in an opportunity for faithful Catholic leadership development presents a teaching moment for lay Catholics who might also be confused or "afraid" of being "brainwashed" by the Catholic Church or its teachings. The above issues are often raised with faithful Catholic organizations because their formation collides with the dominant culture. While there can be prudent concern for organizations that fail to live out the Gospel values of compassion, in this case, it was the Church's teaching on the dignity of marriage, complementarity of the sexes and the beauty of God's plan for the family, that was considered "ultra-conservative" and "anti-gay, anti-women, and anti-compassion."

The Catholic Church has been around for nearly 2,000 years. It is older than any political ideology or economic model in existence today. It is a lot older than the two political parties in the United States. It is much older than the original Civil Rights movement, and older than any of the new issues today labeled as civil rights issues. The Catholic Church is also much older than Karl Max and Adam Smith. It was around before we knew or understood the current, left-right political spectrum society seems split up on.

The Catholic Church is more than an organization; it is a living organism, who carries within itself the Truth as revealed by God and the cumulative human wisdom of its members—saints and sinners—through the centuries. Additionally, and most importantly, it carries within it the divine wisdom of the Holy Spirit, which has guided the Church and its teachings from its inception until now. The Church is a master teacher in humanity!

While we understand that some today try to pit the Church into a corner, have Her choose a "side," the Church will always be above this, because the Church will always be about the Truth. And the most compassionate thing a human being can do for another will always be to speak with Truth, about anything. Furthermore, the Catholic Church is anti-sin, not anti-anybody. We often tell children when they use the word "hate" to refer to something trivial, "you don't hate that, you dislike it or disagree with it." Indeed, a Catholic who understands and lives his or her Faith can only hate two things: the devil and sin. That is the true Church, which always approaches the topic of sin with compassion because we are all sinners.

As part of our call to faithfulness, we are called to unity. Divisive terms, like "types of Catholics" create a split in the Church that should not be there. All the baptized are children of God, and we are all one Church. So unless we are referring to the three states of the Church—the Church Militant refers to all Catholics on Earth, the Church Penitent to those in Purgatory, and the Church Triumphant to the saints in Heaven—there are really only two "types" of Catholics: those who understand and practice their Faith in adherence with *all* of the teachings of the Church, and those who do not.

God is Love, but He is also the Way, the Truth, and the Life. Truth is compassion, in its most honest form. Indeed, what Catholics do when trying to become a different "type," other than faithful, is reject God and the truths of His Church. Every time we make room for or accommodate public opinion, today's lifestyles, or the most prevalent political stances in any given issue, at the expense of God's Truth, we are making less room for His Truth in our lives.

So, in our final analysis, the Catholic Church is not out to brainwash anyone. We authors certainly are not "pressurizing" anyone or using "forcible means." And we aren't teaching anything that to a faithful and practicing Catholic should come across as "radically different beliefs." We are teaching the Catholic Faith, and how it is lived out fully—practically and passionately—as leaders in civil society. Today unfortunately, there are too many false Catholic groups and even a false Gospel in circulation. This is not new to the Church. The remedy to disobedience is not new, either. Ultimately, we must go seek faithfulness to the true Church and its teachings. Let's go back to Jesus, His true Church and His teachings.

We find much inspiration in the following words of Bishop Olmsted, when he was faced with criticism for having to remove the Catholic designation of an important hospital which had performed an abortion: "Whether I am looked at one way or another, if I am given praise or whether I am given ridicule, it doesn't matter. What I am called to be is faithful to Jesus Christ and His Church."[83]

Chapter 15
Identity and Purpose

Don't let your life be barren. Be useful. Make yourself felt. Shine forth with the torch of your faith and your love.

With your apostolic life, wipe out the trail of filth and slime left by the corrupt sowers of hatred. And set aflame all the ways of the earth with the fire of Christ that you bear in your heart.[84]

Catholic leadership for civil society should ultimately be about holiness. It is about sanctifying ourselves by sanctifying the world around us. Most people go through life not understanding who they are and what they were made for. If you are a Catholic professional, who aspires to be a leader for civil society, we want you to understand that you are a child of God before anything else. Out of that understanding flows the understanding of your purpose in life: you were made for holiness, for Heaven. We are convinced that there are two fundamental areas where many Catholic professionals struggle today: identity and purpose.

The most essential question in life: who are you?

Of course, you have an answer, but we are looking for something deeper than your given name. This is the most essential question in life because your answer determines everything else. What is at the heart of this question? Identity! This question is one that most people needed to suffer through—a lot—before they found the adequate answer. Through struggles, we come to realize that not all the money in the world, not a college education, not a career, nor your level of skills, none of it means anything if you don't know who you are. If you are not there yet, we hope God will reveal to you who it is you are—your true identity as His son or daughter—and what that means for your life.

Today some of you—influenced by the culture—are tempted to build an identity around things such as sports, your taste in music, cars, motorcycles, traveling, golf, hunting, a particular political party, your professional career, your country of origin, even your ethnicity. But the truth is that while these things might be personal preferences, aspects of your life, or even part of your identity, none of them are the real you.

So, who are you? Well, at the most basic level you are a human being. A creature, with intellect and will, and dignity above all creatures. And if you are a baptized Christian, then you are an adopted child of God. Because of those reasons, your life is very valuable. That is who you are, at the very core. That is the real you. The other stuff is superficial, even a distraction from your true identity.

We don't know your stories, but if you are reading these lines we hope someone or perhaps a series of events have given you the gift of a Catholic Faith. That is your compass! If you have made it this far, we are guessing you view your Faith as such. There are too many 40-, 60- and 80-year-olds who have wasted their entire lives without knowing who they are or what they were made for. Let's endeavor to *not* be those men and women. Furthermore, if you are in the professional world, we invite you to join us in the adventure of becoming a virtuous leader, rooted in your identity as a child of God. Let us become the Catholic leaders that civil society so desperately needs today, rooted in who we are and what we were created for.

We've all heard the paraphrased words, originally in German, by Pope Benedict XVI, given to a group of young people. He said "the world offers you comfort, but you were not made for comfort. You were made for greatness!" What is this greatness he was referring to? The greatness of a lifelong commitment to building character, based on the search for Truth, Goodness, and Beauty, a lifelong commitment to develop your own character through continued growth in prudence, courage, justice and self-control. These are the foundations that can turn you into a virtuous leader, one who can reclaim Christendom. That's what you were made for!

Ladies and gentlemen, be careful. Some of you have made a little money and tasted success, and this often pulls you away from your call to greatness, obsessed by things that have absolutely no value. And we don't just see this among the wealthy. We see it in the barrios, men who work double shifts, only to put on their cars the most expensive rims or wear the most expensive jewelry. Or even worse, we've seen people give up a life of hard work and exchange it for the false, easy life of organized crime or corruption. Why do they do these things? Because they don't know who they are. And they don't know what they were made for.

Like many of you, we authors come from working families. We know how much you and your families have suffered, because life is not easy. If that is you, we know of the sacrifices your parents made to get you to where you are. That's for the ones who had two parents, because often, in today's modern society (even within the Church), it's a single mom or dad, who sacrifices everything to raise the children and give them a better future. We know that in our Catholic communities, there is a lot of pain and suffering, and in spite of the sincere effort of many and the beautiful example they give, there is hardly such a thing as the perfect family.

If you were given the gift of the Catholic Faith, you face the prospect of doing something great with your life. To do this, you must never forget who you are. First and foremost, commit to honor the dignity conferred onto you by your Creator and the sacrifice His Son made for you at the cross. Then, go on and be a doctor, engineer, or teacher. Join a board or two. Be a Catholic leader in civil society! But that can't define who you are, that can only be another gift for you to share with others. So, become the best doctor, the best engineer, the best teacher you can be by treating others with compassion, love and respect, because you will recognize in them the inherent dignity of every human being. Become the Catholic leader God wants you to be.

The next time somebody asks you about the two most confusing concepts of our times—identity and purpose—we want you to tell them who you are: you are a child of God, and what you were made for: holiness. Brothers and sisters, our Father is calling us to a dramatic transformation. He is calling us to be saints, sanctifying ourselves by sanctifying the world as Catholic leaders in civil society. Do not let that opportunity pass.

We hope the vision, resources and advice provided through this book can become a roadmap for you in the journey to become a Catholic leader for civil society. Remember, "you were not made for comfort; you were made for greatness." And any greatness is worthless if it does not flow from our true identity as sons and daughters of God in Our Lord Jesus Christ. Let's go forth and reclaim the world for Him!

Appendix
Recommended Further Reading

VATICAN II DOCUMENTS

You may visit http://www.vatican.va/archive/hist_councils/ii_vatican_council/index.htm for a full list of the Vatican II documents.

FOUNDATIONAL DOCUMENTS OF CATHOLIC SOCIAL TEACHING

You may visit https://www.usccb.org/beliefs-and-teachings/what-we-believe/catholic-social-teaching/foundational-documents for a full list of the foundational documents of Catholic Social Teaching. Below are several documents pertaining to the topics of this book.

Papal and Vatican Documents
Rerum Novarum (On the Condition of Labor)—Pope Leo XIII, 1891
Gaudium et Spes (Pastoral Constitution on the Church in the Modern World)—Second Vatican Council, 1965
Dignitatis Humanae (Declaration on Religious Freedom)—Second Vatican Council, 1965
Compendium of the Social Doctrine of the Church—Pontifical Council for Justice and Peace, 2004
Laudato Si' (On Care for Our Common Home)—Pope Francis, 2015
Evangelii Gaudium (The Joy of the Gospel)—Pope Francis, 2013
Caritas in Veritate (Charity in Truth)—Pope Benedict XVI, 2009
Centesimus Annus (The Hundredth Year)—St. John Paul II, 1991
Sollicitudo Rei Socialis (On Social Concern)—St. John Paul II, 1987
Evangelium Vitae (The Gospel of Life)—St. John Paul II, 1995
Mater et Magistra (Christianity and Social Progress)—St. John XXIII, 1961

Laborem Exercens (On Human Work)—St. John Paul II, 1981
Octogesima Adveniens (A Call to Action)—St. Pope Paul VI, 1971
Populorum Progressio (On the Development of Peoples)—St. Paul VI, 1967
Pacem in Terris (Peace on Earth)—St. John XXIII, 1963

United States Catholic Bishops Documents
Economic Justice for All, November 1986
A Catholic Framework for Economic Life, November 1996
Forming Consciences for Faithful Citizenship, November 2015, November 2011, November 2007

CATECHISM OF THE CATHOLIC CHURCH

The *Catechism of the Catholic Church* is a complete summary of the teachings of the Catholic Church. The *Catechism* draws from the Bible, the Mass, the Sacraments, Church tradition and the lives of the saints to present the fullness of the truth of the Catholic Faith. It presents a comprehensive list of challenges and answers to those challenges.

BUSINESS DINING ETIQUETTE

We recommend reading the following document published by the Career Services Center at the University of Delaware for a complete list and comprehensive understanding of how to conduct oneself during business meals and meetings.

https://my.lerner.udel.edu/wp-content/uploads/BusinessDiningEtiquette.pdf.

References

[1] Pope John Paul II. "Address to the Council of European Episcopal Conferences," October 11, 1985.

[2] Josemaría Escrivá. *Furrow* (London-New York: Scepter, 1987), No. 8.

[3] Father Mike Schmitz, "The Pennsylvania Sex Abuse Scandal," YouTube, August 22, 2018, video, 16:33, https://www.youtube.com/watch?v=AdR8eyaDCHg.

[4] Leon Bloy, *La Femme Pauvre* (France: Le Livre de Poche, 1964).

[5] Archbishop Fulton J. Sheen, "Address to the Knights of Columbus," June 1972.

[6] Josemaría Escrivá. *Furrow* (London-New York: Scepter, 1987), No. 395.

[7] *Oxford Advanced Learner's Dictionary*, s.v. "Leadership."

[8] Ps. 145:3-7 NABRE

[9] Josemaría Escrivá. *Friends of God* (London: Scepter, 1981), No. 60.

[10] Josemaría Escrivá. *The Way* (New York: All Saints Press, 1963), No. 602.

[11] Second Vatican Council, *Lumen* Gentium. The Holy See, accessed January 2021, https://www.vatican.va/archive/hist_councils/ii_vatican_council/documents/vat-ii_const_19641121_lumen-gentium_en.html.

[12] Pope John Paul II. "Address of John Paul II to Participants in the International Interview Promoted by the French School of Rome." Speech, May 30, 1986.

[13] Second Vatican Council, *Dei Verbum*. The Holy See, accessed January 2021, https://www.vatican.va/archive/hist_councils/ii_vatican_council/documents/vat-ii_const_19651118_dei-verbum_en.html.

[14] Second Vatican Council, *Dei Verbum*. The Holy See, accessed January 2021, https://www.vatican.va/archive/hist_councils/ii_vatican_council/documents/vat-ii_const_19651118_dei-verbum_en.html.

[15] Second Vatican Council, *Dei Verbum*. The Holy See, accessed January 2021, https://www.vatican.va/archive/hist_councils/ii_vatican_council/documents/vat-ii_const_19651118_dei-verbum_en.html.

[16] Matt. 28:19-20 NABRE

[17] Second Vatican Council, *Lumen* Gentium. The Holy See, accessed January 2021, https://www.vatican.va/archive/hist_councils/ii_vatican_council/documents/vat-ii_const_19641121_lumen-gentium_en.html.

[18] Second Vatican Council, *Lumen* Gentium. The Holy See, accessed January 2021, https://www.vatican.va/archive/hist_councils/ii_vatican_council/documents/vat-ii_const_19641121_lumen-gentium_en.html.

[19] Second Vatican Council, *Lumen* Gentium. The Holy See, accessed January 2021, https://www.vatican.va/archive/hist_councils/ii_vatican_council/documents/vat-ii_const_19641121_lumen-gentium_en.html.

[20] Second Vatican Council, *Lumen* Gentium. The Holy See, accessed January 2021, https://www.vatican.va/archive/hist_councils/ii_vatican_council/documents/vat-ii_const_19641121_lumen-gentium_en.html.

[21] Second Vatican Council, *Apostolicam Actuositatem*. The Holy See, accessed January 2021, https://www.vatican.va/archive/hist_councils/ii_vatican_council/documents/vat-ii_decree_19651118_apostolicam-actuositatem_en.html.

[22] Second Vatican Council, *Apostolicam Actuositatem*. The Holy See, accessed January 2021, https://www.vatican.va/archive/hist_councils/ii_vatican_council/documents/vat-ii_decree_19651118_apostolicam-actuositatem_en.html.

[23] Second Vatican Council, *Apostolicam Actuositatem*. The Holy See, accessed January 2021, https://www.vatican.va/archive/hist_councils/ii_vatican_council/documents/vat-ii_decree_19651118_apostolicam-actuositatem_en.html.

[24] Second Vatican Council, *Apostolicam Actuositatem*. The Holy See, accessed January 2021, https://www.vatican.va/archive/hist_councils/ii_vatican_council/documents/vat-ii_decree_19651118_apostolicam-actuositatem_en.html.

[25] Second Vatican Council, *Apostolicam Actuositatem*. The Holy See, accessed January 2021, https://www.vatican.va/archive/hist_councils/ii_vatican_council/documents/vat-ii_decree_19651118_apostolicam-actuositatem_en.html.

[26] Josemaría Escrivá. *Furrow* (London-New York: Scepter, 1987), No. 414.

[27] Second Vatican Council, *Gaudium et Spes*. The Holy See, accessed February 2021, https://www.vatican.va/archive/hist_councils/ii_vatican_council/documents/vat-ii_const_19651207_gaudium-et-spes_en.html.

[28] Matt. 16:24-25 NABRE

[29] Second Vatican Council, *Gaudium et Spes*. The Holy See, accessed February 2021, https://www.vatican.va/archive/hist_councils/ii_vatican_council/documents/vat-ii_const_19651207_gaudium-et-spes_en.html.

[30] Second Vatican Council, *Gaudium et Spes*. The Holy See, accessed February 2021, https://www.vatican.va/archive/hist_councils/ii_vatican_council/documents/vat-ii_const_19651207_gaudium-et-spes_en.html.

[31] Second Vatican Council, *Gaudium et Spes*. The Holy See, accessed February 2021, https://www.vatican.va/archive/hist_councils/ii_vatican_council/documents/vat-ii_const_19651207_gaudium-et-spes_en.html.

[32] Josemaría Escrivá. *The Way* (New York: All Saints Press, 1963), No. 54.

[33] Josemaría Escrivá. *Furrow* (London-New York: Scepter, 1987), No. 970.

[34] The Holy See, *Catechism of the Catholic Church* (Doubleday, 1995), 9.

[35] Ps. 139: 13-14 NABRE

[36] Jer. 29:11 NABRE

[37] Second Vatican Council, *Gaudium et Spes*. The Holy See, accessed March 2021, https://www.vatican.va/archive/hist_councils/ii_vatican_council/documents/vat-ii_const_19651207_gaudium-et-spes_en.html.

[38] Second Vatican Council, *Gaudium et Spes*. The Holy See, accessed March 2021, https://www.vatican.va/archive/hist_councils/ii_vatican_council/documents/vat-ii_const_19651207_gaudium-et-spes_en.html.

[39] Roxana Amaton. "The Pro-Life Professional," *Tepeyac Leadership Initiative* (blog), March 11, 2021, https://tliprogram.org/2021/03/11/the-pro-life-professional/.

[40] Josemaría Escrivá. *Furrow* (London-New York: Scepter, 1987), No. 860.

[41] Pontifical Council of Justice and Peace. 2006. *Compendium of the Social Doctrine of the Church*. London, England: Burns & Oates.

[42] Pontifical Council of Justice and Peace. 2006. *Compendium of the Social Doctrine of the Church*. London, England: Burns & Oates.

[43] Pontifical Council of Justice and Peace. 2006. *Compendium of the Social Doctrine of the Church*. London, England: Burns & Oates.

[44] Pontifical Council of Justice and Peace. 2006. *Compendium of the Social Doctrine of the Church*. London, England: Burns & Oates.

[45] *Dictionary.com*, s.v. "subsidiarity," accessed April 2021, https://www.dictionary.com/browse/subsidiarity.

[46] Pontifical Council of Justice and Peace. 2006. *Compendium of the Social Doctrine of the Church*. London, England: Burns & Oates.

[47] The Holy See, *Catechism of the Catholic Church* (Doubleday, 1995), 517.

[48] Josemaría Escrivá. *Furrow* (London-New York: Scepter, 1987), No. 789.

[49] Stan Weed, PhD; Irene Erikson, PhD; Russell Gombosi, MD; Michelle Cretella, MD, "School-Based Sex Education in the United States," American College of Pediatricians, American College of Pediatricians, September 2018, https://acpeds.org/position-statements/school-based-sex-education-in-the-united-states.

[50] International Planned Parenthood Federation & World Association for Sexual Health. *Fulfil! Guidance document for the implementation of young people's sexual rights.* 2016. https://www.ippf.org/sites/default/files/2016-09/Fulfil!%20Guidance%20document%20for%20the%20implementation%20of%20young%20people's%20sexual%20rights%20(IPPF-WAS).pdf.

[51] International Planned Parenthood Federation & World Association for Sexual Health. *Fulfil! Guidance document for the implementation of young people's sexual rights.* 2016. https://www.ippf.org/sites/default/files/2016-09/Fulfil!%20Guidance%20document%20for%20the%20implementation%20of%20young%20people's%20sexual%20rights%20(IPPF-WAS).pdf.

[52] International Planned Parenthood Federation & World Association for Sexual Health. *Fulfil! Guidance document for the implementation of young people's sexual rights.* 2016. https://www.ippf.org/sites/default/files/2016-09/Fulfil!%20Guidance%20document%20for%20the%20implementation%20of%20young%20people's%20sexual%20rights%20(IPPF-WAS).pdf.

[53] Pope John Paul II, *Evangelium Vitae* (March 25, 1995), https://www.vatican.va/content/john-paul-ii/en/encyclicals/documents/hf_jp-ii_enc_25031995_evangelium-vitae.html.

[54] Pope John Paul II, *Evangelium Vitae* (March 25, 1995), https://www.vatican.va/content/john-paul-ii/en/encyclicals/documents/hf_jp-ii_enc_25031995_evangelium-vitae.html.

[55] Pope John Paul II, *Evangelium Vitae* (March 25, 1995), https://www.vatican.va/content/john-paul-ii/en/encyclicals/documents/hf_jp-ii_enc_25031995_evangelium-vitae.html.

[56] Pope John Paul II, *Evangelium Vitae* (March 25, 1995), https://www.vatican.va/content/john-paul-ii/en/encyclicals/documents/hf_jp-ii_enc_25031995_evangelium-vitae.html.

[57] Pontifical Council of Justice and Peace. 2014. *Vocation of the Business Leader: A Reflection*. Vatican City: Pontifical Council for Justice and Peace.

[58] *Oxford Advanced Learner's Dictionary*, s.v. "fake news."

[59] Josemaría Escrivá. *Furrow* (London-New York: Scepter, 1987), No. 118.

[60] Graves, Jim, "The man behind Catholic U's largest donation ever," *Catholic World Report* (San Francisco, CA), May 19, 2016. https://www.catholicworldreport.com/2016/05/19/the-man-behind-catholic-us-largest-donation-ever/.

[61] Morris-Young, Dan, "Tim Busch, conservative activist-philanthropist, rejects anti-Francis label," *National Catholic Reporter* (Kansas City, MO), June 12, 2019. https://www.ncronline.org/news/accountability/tim-busch-conservative-activist-philanthropist-rejects-anti-francis-label.

[62] Morris-Young, Dan, "Tim Busch, conservative activist-philanthropist, rejects anti-Francis label," *National Catholic Reporter* (Kansas City, MO), June 12, 2019. https://www.ncronline.org/news/accountability/tim-busch-conservative-activist-philanthropist-rejects-anti-francis-label.

[63] "Saint Gianna Beretta Molla," Franciscan Media, Franciscan Media, April 19, 2021, https://www.franciscanmedia.org/saint-of-the-day/saint-gianna-beretta-molla.

[64] "Saint Gianna Beretta Molla," Franciscan Media, Franciscan Media, April 19, 2021, https://www.franciscanmedia.org/saint-of-the-day/saint-gianna-beretta-molla.

[65] Gianna Beretta Molla and Pietro Molla, *The Journey of Our Love: The Letters of Saint Gianna Beretta and Pietro Molla* (Boston: Pauline Books & Media, 2014)

[66] "Andrew V. Abela Dean and Ordinary Professor of Marketing," The Catholic University of America, accessed August 2021, https://business.catholic.edu/faculty-and-research/faculty-profiles/abela-andrew/index.html.

[67] Borowski, Dave, "A champion of Catholic business ethics," *Arlington Catholic Herald* (Arlington, VA), April 16, 2014. https://www.catholicherald.com/news/local_news/a_champion_of_catholic_business_ethics/.

[68] Borowski, Dave, "A champion of Catholic business ethics," *Arlington Catholic Herald* (Arlington, VA), April 16, 2014. https://www.catholicherald.com/news/local_news/a_champion_of_catholic_business_ethics/.

[69] Nomination of the Honorable Amy Coney Barrett to be an Associate Justice of the Supreme Court of the United States (October 12, 2020).

[70] Coney Barrett, Amy, interview by Stephanie Maloney, *Hillsdale College*, May 21, 2019.

[71] Jim Caviezel, interview by Pete Hegseth, *Fox News*, September 19, 2020.

[72] Jim Caviezel, interview by Pete Hegseth, *Fox News*, September 19, 2020.

[73] Jim Caviezel, interview by Pete Hegseth, *Fox News*, September 19, 2020.

[74] Josemaría Escrivá. *Furrow* (London-New York: Scepter, 1987), No. 968.

[75] Josemaría Escrivá. *The Way* (New York: All Saints Press, 1963), No. 19.

[76] Javier Lopez, "Professional Prestige," Opus Dei, Opus Dei, March 24, 2015, https://opusdei.org/en-us/article/professional-prestige/.

[77] Second Vatican Council, *Apostolicam Actuositatem*. The Holy See, accessed September 2021, https://www.vatican.va/archive/hist_councils/ii_vatican_council/documents/vat-ii_decree_19651118_apostolicam-actuositatem_en.html.

[78] Cristofer Pereyra, "What I Call Dressed for Success," *Tepeyac Leadership Initiative* (blog), November 7, 2019, https://tliprogram.org/2019/11/07/what-i-call-dressed-for-success/.

[79] Javier Lopez, "Professional Prestige," Opus Dei, Opus Dei, March 24, 2015, https://opusdei.org/en-us/article/professional-prestige/.

[80] Josemaría Escrivá. *Friends of God* (London: Scepter, 1981), No. 57.

[81] Josemaría Escrivá. *Friends of God* (London: Scepter, 1981), No. 60.

[82] Josemaría Escrivá. *Furrow* (London-New York: Scepter, 1987), No. 529.

[83] Bishop Thomas Olmsted, "Bishop Olmsted Responds to Blogger Criticism," YouTube, December, 23, 2010, video, 0:51, https://www.youtube.com/watch?v=OsOgpgQXcgQ.

[84] Josemaría Escrivá. *The Way* (New York: All Saints Press, 1963), No. 1.

Made in the USA
Columbia, SC
21 January 2025